HOW TO
PICK A
SPOUSE

DAN CHUN

Revell

a division of Baker Publishing Group
Grand Rapids, Michigan

Published by Revell
a division of Baker Publishing Group
PO Box 6287, Grand Rapids, MI 49516-6287
www.revellbooks.com

Revell edition published 2014
ISBN 978-0-8007-2478-8

Previously published by Regal Books

Printed in the United States of America

The Library of Congress has cataloged the original edition as follows:
    Chun, Dan.
      How to pick a spouse : a proven, practical guide to finding a lifelong partner / Dan Chun.
       pages cm
     ISBN 978-0-8307-6975-9 (trade paper)
      1. Mate selection—Religious aspects—Christianity. 2. Marriage—Religious aspects—Christianity. I. Title.
    BV835.C479 2014
    248.8'4—dc23   2013040133

15   16   17   18   19   20   7   6   5   4   3   2

To my wife, Pam, the love of my life for 33-plus years:
the best decision I have ever made was marrying you.

Contents

Acknowledgments

I am very grateful for the community of friends, loved ones and relatives who helped me in writing this book. Many thanks to Shaunti Feldhahn, who cheered me on to do the book and to do it right. Thanks to Jim White, who did the heavy lifting in getting my thoughts edited, and to Josh Urich, who made my ideas more articulate. I'm also grateful for Thomas Cheong, my original researcher. For my *ohana* (Hawaiian for "family"), who read drafts, helped with research, gave feedback and encouragement, I offer a bouquet of thank-yous (and forgive me if I have forgotten someone):

Andrew, Christine and Elizabeth Brackenbury
Mark and Diane Button
Shirley Cavanagh
Craig and Laura Chan
Valerie Chan
Anne Marie Chun
Noelle Chun
Pam Chun
Vincent Daubenspeck
Paul and Jeannie Edwards
Sharon Fan
Carolyn Grossnickle

Jacqueline Hänschke
Carola Hernandez-Pappas
Dave and Shayna Kusumoto
Kirk Leavy
Scott Makuakane
Arne and Maria Lim
Ron Mathieu
Stella Matsuda
Lauren McCartha
Karl and Sue Miller
Mike Miller
Bob and Patty Moorhead

Darlene Keakalina O'Brien
Vip and Sharon Patel
Ben and Christy Pierce
Elizabeth Pugh
Rosella Shishido
Garrett Sullivan
Susannah Sullivan
Gary Toh
Olivia and Arlin Torbett
Mary Vinson
Kyle Watari
Robin Winterlin

Special thanks to my agent, Kyle Duncan, for believing in me and connecting me with Regal Books. At Regal, I am grateful to Kim Bangs, and a special *mahalo* (Hawaiian for "thank you") to Carol Eide and Julie Carobini for overseeing the editing.

I am forever grateful to First Presbyterian Church of Honolulu for the time to write this and to Menlo Park Presbyterian Church for some of my best ministry years heading up its Singles Ministries Department.

Foreword

As the founder of eHarmony.com, I am asked to read all kinds of books on the subjects of dating and marriage. Our organization has been part of over 600,000 marriages, so people think that if I say it's a good book, then others will read it. I put off reading the manuscript for *How to Pick a Spouse* as long as I could, because I get asked a lot and I get tired of the requests. But this book by Dan Chun was worth my time—I'm really taken with it. Dan Chun is an experienced, dedicated, unbelievably wise and down-to-earth writer. He knows how to be practical both in his encouragement and in his advice.

Let me get right to the point: If you are thinking about getting married, and if you are a Christian, you need to read this book. It will hold your interest; it will inform you like you have not been informed before; and you will end up saying it's one of the best books you've read on this subject in your entire life.

If you apply the principles in this book, you will be able to master the various stages of choosing a spouse in such a way that the likelihood of divorce will simply have a zero probability. Take your time reading *How to Pick a Spouse*, answer all the questions that are posed to you, make sure that you get very clearly in mind what Dan Chun is saying to you, and I guarantee that you will find it both exciting and incredibly helpful.

What is the nature of my guarantee? If you read this book and follow its teachings, and your marriage does not succeed, I will give you a free membership to eHarmony.com. This is the best guarantee that you will ever receive because the conditions of this agreement will keep a negative outcome from ever happening to you and the love of your life. And if you go through this book in a group setting, you will get even more out of it. So I encourage this too.

What else should I say to motivate you to keep reading? First, every person I know who isn't married really needs this book. If you have been married before, and it didn't work out, then you clearly need this book! But if this is your first marriage, and you are highly unpracticed at picking a wife or husband, you are in great danger if you don't follow these wise decision-making principles.

Here's another guarantee! If you read this book and find it uninteresting, write to me. Again, I will give you a free membership to eHarmony.com—but you've got to tell me why you find it uninteresting. Why do I say this? Because *I* found it interesting, and I don't usually like books like this! So take my guarantee one way or another. Read this book, and become informed in a practical way about how to be highly successful in one of the most important endeavors in which you will ever engage. If you do this before you get married to anybody, you will probably thank me for the rest of your life.

By Neil Clark Warren
Founder and CEO of eHarmony.com

Introduction

A good woman is hard to find,
and worth far more than diamonds.

PROVERBS 31:10, *THE MESSAGE*

You either break up or you get married. It's a jarring reality, but once you start dating, those are generally your only two options.

I have a book on my shelf about how to get married within one month; it's more than 100 pages long. If I were to write that book, I would only need one page with this one sentence: *Lower your standards.*

There is no trick to getting married in 30 days. If you lower your standards, you—*anyone*—can get married quickly. Most of us, however, want to get married to the right person at the right time in the right way. Assuming that is what you want, you will need some healthy criteria to help you determine what to look for in a lifelong spouse, so this book is for you.

I want to help people choose the right marriage partner. I want people to avoid divorce. Dating someone and then breaking up is painful and can be scarring; but sadly, breakups are not the only potential for pain. Marriage brings fulfillment—*unless* you choose the wrong person. A wrong choice in a marriage partner can mean a long, painful, unfulfilled marriage and even, potentially, a divorce. In other words, it can mean hell on earth.

A high percentage of people get divorced today—between 20 and 39 percent depending on the demographic.[1] Would you get on an airplane with your spouse and children if you knew there was a 20 to 39 percent chance that the plane would crash? But what if there were a way to improve your chances and fly without that high crash risk?

I wrote this book to increase your chances of finding a long, fulfilling marriage and to prevent a painful, unnecessary divorce. Whether you are in college or you're an older adult; whether you are currently dating someone and thinking about marriage or you've been divorced and are thinking about how to choose better next time, this book is for you. You may even want to give it to someone else to read or use it in a group and discuss the issues presented. You'll find discussion starter questions at the end of each chapter for use in a group or for your own personal reflection.

People who have applied the principles in this book to their search for a life partner have experienced a drastically lower divorce rate: *Only 9.5 percent got divorced over the last 20 years.* (I know this because out of the 261 singles who married during or soon after the time of my singles ministry, only 25 had divorced 20-plus years later—that equals 14 divorces out of 143 marriages.) An approximate 9 percent divorce rate is nearly 110 percent better than the best national statistical average and more than 300 percent better than the high end of the scale!

But, alas, I am getting ahead of myself. Let's look at the terrain of probabilities and challenges. In order to fully appreciate the need for a practical course in selecting a spouse, you have to understand the high degree of difficulty in having a marriage that lasts a lifetime.

It is true that depending on the demographics of a population (ethnicity, age, finances, location and so on), 20 to 39 percent of marriages end in divorce. And if it's your second or third marriage, there's a higher probability that you may divorce. A marriage that remains intact even in the face of physical violence or emotional and verbal abuse can be torturous. And for some who stay in a bad marriage, silence due to incompatibility can almost be as bad as physical or verbal abuse. So choosing the wrong spouse and staying in a bad marriage is painful, even without the hurt and devastation of divorce.

Therefore, it is critical to choose the right spouse. This book is primarily practical in nature. No lofty principles or head-in-the-clouds ideas, just the nitty-gritty of courtship and marriage.

If you are a Christian, you can pray, and hope that God will lead you to the right person; but if you are not *practical* in your search, all the prayer in the world might not do any good. We can't be so idealistic and heavenly minded that we're of no earthly good.

To be sure, the current concept of "dating" is a relatively new phenomenon in Western culture. It only started in the 1900s, when American society began to abandon the practice of arranged marriage for practical reasons and made married love the primary focus of people's emotional satisfaction. In the old world, there were numerous social rules and chaperonage. Outings were highly controlled. There were more processes and rules and research to make sure a date was a good fit for someone. Dates required that a man and a woman have the *socially approved* right to even "ask someone out on a date." It was only just the two of them if chaperones didn't accompany them.

But that began to change in the early twentieth century. With that change came a new threat to the family that brought a greater potential for divorce. Emphasis on romantic love as opposed to a relationship based on commitment and approval by the two families unintentionally eroded marriages and increased the chances of divorce. Romantic love, for many, became so feelings-focused and preoccupied with sex and immediate gratification that over time some of the good logic and rationale in choosing a spouse got lost.

Stephanie Coontz makes the point in her epic book *Marriage, A History*:

> The people who took idealization of love and intimacy to new heights during the nineteenth century did not intend to shake up marriage or unleash a new preoccupation with sexual gratification. They meant to strengthen marriage by encouraging husbands and wives to weave new emotional bonds. In the long run, however, they weakened it. The focus on romantic love eventually undercut the doctrine of separate spheres for men and women and the ideal of female purity, putting new strains on the institution of marriage. . . . In the seventeenth and

eighteenth centuries even the most enthusiastic advocates of love matches had believed that love developed after one had selected a suitable prospective mate. People didn't fall in love. They tiptoed into it.[2]

Even though dating today seems to be a free-for-all rather than "tiptoeing," there are indeed some principles to follow that can help you beat the odds and find a spouse for a lifetime. The principles outlined in this book, while not as stifling as Victorian-era social rules, will nevertheless take some of the guesswork out of picking a spouse.

Why Should I Listen to You, Dan Chun?

Here are seven reasons why you should listen to me:

1. *I have been a pastor for 35 years.* That's more than three decades of counseling single and married people. I have heard their stories, heartbreaks and hopes. I have worked with countless couples in premarital counseling. I have helped pick up the pieces by providing posttraumatic care when a marriage dissolves. With such a breadth of experience, I have been able to see that there are *patterns* to what works and what does not work when picking a spouse.
2. *For six-and-a-half years, I specialized in pastoral ministry to more than 5,000 single adults of all ages—never married, separated, divorced and widowed.* There are few pastors in this country who have had such a unique, prolonged, exclusive care for singles. Like a specialty in medicine, I have had a chance to study the unique nature of singleness and how to prepare singles for marriage. The wisdom I share is rooted in long-term experience of singles' issues. I will use real-life case stories to demonstrate some of my points. Names have been changed (unless I have permission to use a name), but the stories are real.

3. *The principles I taught as a pastor to singles, to prepare them for spouse-selection, worked.* Out of the 261 singles that got married around the time of my singles ministry, only 25 were divorced 20-plus years later! That's only a 9.5 percent divorce rate. With such a drastic difference from the national average—a 110-plus percent improvement on the *best* statistics, 300-plus percent improvement on the *worst*—it is clear that these principles are worth trying. Chance or luck could not account for such a huge difference.

4. *All of the guidelines and principles I present in this book are consistent with the theology of the Bible, which I believe is one of the few reliable, time-tested, ethical-moral-divine manuscripts in the world.* These principles have been proven to work for centuries. The Bible is our best guide—not the Kardashian family; not Barney Stinson (played by Neil Patrick Harris) on TV's *How I Met Your Mother,* where Barney's bachelor goal in life was to sleep with as many women as possible and have a place to live within 23 minutes of meeting women so he could get them to bed quickly. The Bible has imparted wisdom and practicality to those who have availed themselves of its truths. It's just that most of us have not read it; even those who have read it rarely derive from it principles for dating. Even if you're not Christian, you can still agree that the fly-by-night morality of pop culture is not the stuff on which to build a family. While you may not see the Bible as divine in origin, perhaps you can see it as a really old book that wouldn't be around anymore unless it had something good to offer.

5. *The practical steps I teach from Scripture are relevant today.* You might say, "But you taught these principles as a singles pastor back in the 1980s and 1990s. Things are much different now." Oh, really? Not only do we face the same temptations, stresses, heartaches, selfishness, desires and addictions today as singles did 20 and 30 years ago, but those temptations are also

the same as people faced in the first century. These temptations and stresses may come in different forms, but they are all branches from the same tree. As I continue to teach nationally and internationally, I can attest that the questions, doubts, insecurities and peer pressures are the same today as yesterday. As I listen to singles of all ages, their issues and challenges are still the same. The pain of divorce is the same today as it was 25 years ago. Breaking up is still a gut-wrenching experience.

6. *I was once divorced.* I have gone through *two* seasons of being single. I got married early out of college and then divorced at 25, leaving me single again. I know and have felt firsthand the pain, sorrow, low self-esteem, doubts, difficulties and hopes of a single person who was once divorced. I wrote this book out of my empathy, wisdom and personal experience. Apart from my years of experience as a pastor, I learned these lessons of what to do and not to do from the school of hard knocks.

7. *I have been married for more than 30 years.* I know what it takes to find a good spouse and enjoy a marriage that lasts. Yes, it is challenging, but I do know how to find the person with the building blocks to make a good marriage—not the perfect marriage, but a good one. I understand the intricacies of marriage and what it takes to hang in there and flourish for a lifetime.

Did number 6 surprise you? It certainly took me by surprise. Let me explain the circumstances of my divorce so that you can better see where I'm coming from. The divorce happened when I went to seminary.

I was preparing to go into full-time vocational ministry. After a few years of marriage, my wife and I flew to Pasadena, California, to attend Fuller seminary. Just before classes began, my wife said, "I don't love you. In fact, I never loved you." Those words hurt so much. I was devastated. My self-esteem sank so low that I felt like I would have had no problem walking under a closed door. I cried; I despaired; my confidence was shaken to the core. I had come from a family that had never known divorce, and from a faith where, if marriage was hard, you rolled up your sleeves and made it work. I was completely unprepared for the effects of a failed marriage. For years, I had to work on betrayal and abandonment issues.

Being in seminary made it even harder for me due to embarrassment of being in a community of what I assumed were super-mature Christians. No one, let alone a pastor, should get divorced. Pastors were supposed to be role models of family and marriage, and my divorce led some of my friends to question my future plans to be a pastor. My home church had just prayed over me and publicly commissioned me to go off to seminary. Talk about shame! Humiliation cascaded over me.

I tried to make our relationship work, but after two weeks of emergency counseling, and just two weeks before classes began, she left for her out-of-state home. I didn't know many people in my new city 2,500 miles from home. The distance from most of my friends and family made it even harder. Fortunately, one of my first classes required me to be in a small group of fellow seminarians that met every week. That saved my life. They encouraged me. I also formed friendships with a community of Christians who all lived in one house, and they would regularly invite me to dinner. Faculty checked in on me and invited me to meals. As Charles Dickens once wrote, "It was the best of times, it was the worst of times."[3]

Months later, the night before the final exam in my New Testament Survey class, I received the legal divorce papers. I was so distraught that when I took the exam the next day, I got an F. A month after the divorce was final, she married someone I hadn't even known existed. To put it mildly, my seminary years were wilderness years.

I don't want anyone to go through the same kind of pain I experienced. If that can be avoided by choosing wisely, then why not make those choices? The breakup of a dating relationship is painful, but the breakup of a marriage is crushing. A divorce is soul tearing, like the ripping apart of two pieces of paper that are glued together with superglue. There are no easy divorces. Fortunately for me, we didn't have any children; but imagine the suffering if we had? Not only is divorce more difficult when there are children involved, but also the impact of divorce on children can last a long time, and maybe even a lifetime. Research from Judith Wallerstein shows that children of divorced parents are scarred for the rest of their lives.[4]

Unlike the death of a spouse, a divorce can be uniquely more difficult. It's like the American horror film *Night of the Living Dead*. Unlike a physical death, a divorced person may continue to see the spouse who has rejected him or her. Reminders of rejection, betrayal or the relationship-gone-bad can be hauntingly traumatic on a recurring basis. And if there are children to be divided between homes, or shared on a set schedule, it can be even more complex and painful.

So where do you turn for help and guidance to find someone who would be a candidate for lifetime marriage?

Does the Bible Give Us Models for Dating?

To be perfectly honest, the Bible records few examples of weddings, but a lot of bad exhibits of marriage and really bad models of dating. For courtship and dating, the Bible's stories are almost crazy humorous, and we would certainly not want to replicate such romantic encounters. Consider these examples in Scripture (my paraphrase):

- Samson to his parents: "Hey, I met this girl at a party. I have the hots for her. Get her for me!" (See Judges 14:2.)
- Abraham to servant: "Slave, go find my son, Isaac, a wife" (See Genesis 24:2-4.)
- Jacob to Laban: "I saw your daughter Rachel at the well and after one kiss I am madly in love. I want to marry her. What's that? What do you mean, 'You have to work 14 years for me'?" (Read the story in Genesis 29.)

- Ruth: "Boaz can be my sugar daddy! I'll slip into his bedroom at night and wait for him to notice me!" (See Ruth 3:7.)
- Hosea to God: "Say what? I have to go out and marry a prostitute?" (See Hosea 1:2.)
- Solomon: "Hey, God, one wife is not enough. So how does 700 wives and 300 friends-with-benefits sound?" (See 1 Kings 11:3.)
- David: "What do you mean, three strikes and I'm out?! What's wrong with lusting after Bathsheba, killing her husband and lying?" (See 2 Samuel 11:1-27.)

When you read these examples of courtship in the Bible (and there are others), it makes your head spin! What is important to note is that the Bible is not so much a list of dos and don'ts, but a map to a clear pathway where you will want to walk. Everyone needs to set his or her priorities, guidelines and personal mission statement. And a spouse should fit into those goals and passions. But do you even know what goals are worth establishing and seeking? Before you can do that, you need to clarify your personal life vision.

The Three Ms

Not that I have already obtained this or have already reached the goal; but I press on to make it my own, because Christ Jesus has made me his own (Philippians 3:12).

I believe that three of the most important decisions in life are Mate, Mission and Master.

- Mate: Who will be my spouse?
- Mission: What is my purpose or passion in life?
- Master: To whom will I dedicate my life? To Jesus Christ or to someone (or something) else?

I realize that not everyone may want to get married; but since you are reading this book, figuring out your Mate has to be one of the biggest decisions you will ever make.

When I went through a divorce, my Mate and my Mission were in disarray and confusion. It was hard to hear the words of the Master—Jesus. However, there is always hope. When we make wise choices about our Mate, Mission and Master, life can only improve. We experience congruency with God's will. Even if you are reading this book after messing up past relationships, there is always a new chapter to write, if you are willing. You can triumph over tragedy.

God has redeemed me in so many ways. He has taken me from feeling like a zero to feeling like a hero. It's amazing to look back now and to clearly see that God is a God of redemption and transformation.

- Five years after my divorce, I got married again. I have been married to Pam, by God's grace, for more than 33 years. We have three children.
- Thirty years ago, Pam and I founded a leadership-training ministry called Hawaiian Islands Ministries (HIM). The faculty is a list of who's who in Christianity in terms of thought-leaders and Kingdom builders. Every year, 4,000 people gather to hear some of the best Christian communicators in the world offer 100 seminars and lead 6 large worship sessions at our conference (www.himon line.org). We have teamed together to train more than 50,000 leaders. HIM also has a strong social justice wing. We have helped to get 5,000 children released from poverty, in Jesus' name, through child sponsorship with Compassion International (www.compassion.com). Pam is a ministry partner with me. I love her dearly. We share many things in common. First Presbyterian Church of Honolulu (I host a video tour of it at www.fpchawaii.org) is a bit offbeat as it owns, operates and worships at the 242-acre Ko'olau Golf Club (www.koolaugolfclub.com), and manages Ko'olau Ballrooms and Conference Center (www.koolauballrooms.com). Pam and I have served this

church for more than 25 years and HIM for more than 30 years as our Mission. In Pam, I found my Mate who shares in my Mission and follows my Master.

- As for those people who said I should not be a pastor due to the divorce—by God's grace, I have been a pastor for more than three decades and love it. For the last 20 years, I've been the pastor of a church that is in the top 1 percent in size in my denomination of nearly 11,000 churches. The congregation is vital, healthy, growing and fun. It's a great Mission. God is using this so-called "loser" of seminary!

- What about that *F* I got on my exam? Well, the same seminary that gave me the *F* asked me to be on its board of trustees. Talk about zero to hero! This is redemption by the Lord of the Second Chance. All of it is His amazing grace. I am proud to serve Fuller Theological Seminary, the largest nondenominational seminary in North America, and maybe in the world.

Through it all, I decided that my devotion to my Master—Jesus Christ—would be unwavering. He sustained me, strengthened me and gave me endurance and wisdom from above.

My favorite verse from the Bible is Isaiah 41:10 because it has been so true for me. God says, "Do not fear, for I am with you, Do not be afraid, for I am your God; I will strengthen you, I will help you, I will uphold you with my victorious right hand."

I decided that my Mission would be full-time ministry—which is an option for anyone who would see his or her job or avocation as the Mission. You don't have to go to seminary or serve in a church to make full-time work for God your Mission. You can do that wherever you are. Each person must identify his or her passion—his or her purpose or Mission—and then determine how to fulfill it. It might be fulfilled in whatever job you have—teacher, businessperson, secretary, county worker, homemaker and more.

I began this section by defining the Three *M*s—Mate, Mission, Master—as three of the most important life decisions you will ever make, and not necessarily in that order. Obviously, this book focuses on the choice of your Mate. But unless you also define your Master and then your Mission, you will have a difficult time choosing the right Mate. It is critical to choose all three *Ms* wisely.

To give you a better idea of where the principles in this book come from, I invite you to read on and consider the strange case of the singles ministry of Menlo Park Presbyterian Church.

Study Questions

1. How do you feel about the high divorce rate today? Hopeless? Desperate? Determined to do it better?

   _____

   _____

   _____

   _____

2. What would you say are contributing factors to the breakup of a marriage?

   _____

   _____

   _____

   _____

   _____

3. Have you ever carried baggage from one relationship into the next? What do you wish you had left behind?

   _____

   _____

   _____

   _____

   _____

4. In Isaiah 41:10, God says, "Do not fear, for I am with you, do not be afraid, for I am your God; I will strengthen you, I will help you. I will uphold you with my victorious right hand." How does that declaration make you feel?

_____

_____

_____

_____

_____

5. Which of the three *Ms* have you already decided on—Mate, Mission, Master? How do you think that decision could affect the other two?

_____

_____

_____

_____

_____

Notes
1. "New Marriage and Divorce Statistics," The Barna Group, March 31, 2008.
2. Stephanie Coontz, *Marriage, A History* (New York: Penguin Group, 2005), p. 178.
3. Charles Dickens, *A Tale of Two Cities*.
4. Judith S. Wallerstein, Julia M. Lewis, Sandra Blakeslee, *The Unexpected Legacy of Divorce: The 25 Year Landmark Study* (New York: Hyperion, 2000).

I

The Strange Case of the Menlo Park Singles

Seek the Kingdom of God above all else, and live righteously, and he will give you everything you need.

MATTHEW 6:33

There were only about 25,000 people living in the tiny town of Menlo Park, California, in 1985. Nestled in the northern part of Silicon Valley, right at the time the technology and computer industries were taking off, a singles department at Menlo Park Presbyterian Church began to meet. Situated 30 minutes south of the city of San Francisco, and 30 minutes north of the city of San Jose, the church had a reach to more than a million people.

That same year, I was asked to join the staff of Menlo Park Presbyterian Church as an associate pastor to create what was starting to become in vogue: a singles ministries department. We were one of the first churches in the nation to have a department and a pastor dedicated to singles—the never-married, the divorced and the widowed. While churches traditionally have a youth pastor or maybe a children's ministries director, I was to become this church's first "Pastor with Singles." The preposition "with" was carefully chosen. I wasn't going to lord *over* them or be *below* them. Nor was I going to be a pastor *to* or *for* them—I wasn't going to do everything for them while they sat and watched. Rather, I would work *with* them as a coach.

We started building lay leadership teams to offer singles ministries to a variety of singles demographics—young adults, middle-aged singles, older singles, divorced, widowed, blended families, single parents. Within just three years, by God's grace, we had thousands of singles attending our church. While many of them were energetic, enthusiastic about life, passionate to do good and ambitious to serve, some felt broken, misunderstood, judged or abandoned by other churches or by society, or they were looking for a safe place to meet other singles.

At one point, this older, traditional Presbyterian church had more singles attending than married people. The church grew to 3,500 people. Once, when a newcomer came to one of our events and asked me, "Where can I find a woman to lay?" I told him this was not the place for him, and he left. We would say that it was okay for the ministry to be a "meet market," but not a "meat market." We were trying to create a safe place for singles to meet and not have to go to bars or dance clubs.

Former women's Bible Study Fellowship teacher Patti Pierce and our able administrative assistant Rhoda Jackson joined the staff, and the ministry took off. Every week we provided social events, recovery groups and Bible studies attended by 650 people. There were 2,000 to 3,000 people on our mailing list, and we updated it regularly.

During that time, from 1985 to 1992, we taught certain principles about how to pick the right spouse. Those principles were, for the most part, agreed on by the lay leadership and the singles during those wonderful years. Something startling happened, and the seeds planted during those years bore much fruit. More than 20 years later, we took stock of the fruit and were astounded by what we discovered.

The Amazing Statistics

Let all who are spiritually mature agree on these things (Philippians 3:15, *NLT*).

I left Menlo Park in 1991, after serving there for six-and-a half years, when my dad unexpectedly died in Hawaii, and I returned to take care of my mom. Patti Pierce left a year or so later. But many of the singles stayed on for years. Recently the lay leaders from that group and I compiled a list of all those who got married between 1985 and 1995. Then we listed all those who were still married, and those who had divorced or died.

The results were that 261 people got married during that 10-year period. Nearly 20 years later, *more than 90 percent were still married.* Or to put it another way, only 25 were divorced. That's just 9.5 percent! Still another way to look at it: Only 14 marriages out of 143 ended in divorce over a 20-year time frame (9.7 percent).

Before we go further, I need to jump in here and debunk the popular notion that 50 percent of marriages end in divorce. That is misleading. The number is still incredibly high, but not that high. Someone looked at all of the marriages recorded in the U.S. Census that happened in a year and noticed that the divorces that year were half of that number and made the erroneous conclusion that half of all marriages end in divorce. The assumption went viral. But it's not 50 percent. So what is the real divorce rate?

According to a March 31, 2008, report by the Barna Group (entitled "New Marriage and Divorce Statistics Released"), 4 out of every 5 adults (78 percent) get married at least once, and interestingly, born-again Christians get married even more (84 percent). The study found that, among adults who get married, 33 percent divorce at least once. To be more exact, it depends on your demographic. The Barna report said that if you were *not* a college graduate and made less than $20,000, the divorce rate for a first-time marriage was about 39 percent. However, if you were a college graduate with an annual household income of $75,000, the divorce rate for a first-time marriage was 22 percent. And it's further down to 20 percent if you are Asian, notes Barna. To put it together with all demographics, Barna says the national average is about a 1 in 3 chance of divorce.[1]

A Centers for Disease Control report seems to indicate that a second marriage, for some demographics, has a higher chance of divorce.[2] This is verified in research for Shaunti Feldhahn's book *Good News About Marriage.*[3] For my Menlo Park Church Singles Survey, 8 out of the 14 divorces involved people in their second or third marriage; but with such a small pool, that certainly is not predictive. Nevertheless, of the 122 singles who married for the second or third time, more than 100 are still married!

Whatever report you use, Menlo Park's rate of 9.5 percent after a 20-year span is still shockingly low. It is less than half the national divorce rate of even the most optimistic demographics and studies that report a 22 to 45 percent divorce rate. That's a 110 to 473 percent better rating than the best or worst national average.

The Plane to Los Angeles (The *Lost* Effect)

The TV show *Lost*, which ran from 2004–2010, was filmed in Hawaii. This top-running show mesmerized a nation about how passengers survived for years on a "deserted" island after their plane crashed. One day when I got on a flight to Los Angeles, six of the *Lost* cast were on the plane and sitting next to me. I had kind of an eerie feeling when I thought of those characters who got on an airplane doomed to crash. Two rows in front of me, I saw a friend who had been shot down in Vietnam while flying a fighter jet. (This could make a person a bit uneasy during takeoff.)

Now, how would you feel if you got on an airplane from Honolulu to Los Angeles and the airline attendant told you there was a 20 to 39 percent chance the plane would crash and burn (the same odds of a marriage ending in divorce)? But, she says, you could have at least a 90 percent chance of making it all the way to Honolulu if you follow certain directions.

Well, this book will give you those directions. It is all about *not* crashing and burning in the flight known as marriage.

Years ago, I heard about a person who received a federal grant to create a curriculum that would teach engaged couples how to stay married. His outcome showed that the divorce rate for them was *worse* than the national average. That was when I began to wonder if what we had taught during those Menlo Park years would be helpful for others to consider before they dated, or as they dated, *so that more successful marriages would be created.* Healthier marriages result in healthier families. Healthier families result in healthier communities. Healthier communities build healthier countries, which build a better world.

Before we look at the specific tools that made the Menlo Park Singles successful, let's take a look at the jagged edge where some marriages fall off the cliff into divorce. The canyon of suffering is long, dark and deep.

The Disease of Divorce

I love being married. It's so great to find that one
special person you want to annoy for
the rest of your life.
Rita Rudner, comedian and actress

The U.S. Census reports that in 2009 there were a little more than a million divorces in the United States. Let's say the average couple has an average of two children. In that case, in one year, 4 million people are affected by divorce. Now let's say there are four parents-in-law. Now you have 8 million affected in one year by divorce, and that's not counting friends, other relatives and colleagues.

What about the toll on the divorced parents and children? What about the financial toll of missed days of work and school; the therapy; the depression? Much of the work of psychologist and author Judith Wallerstein and her peers show that there are *lifelong* repercussions for most children of divorced parents. Those children carry feelings of abandonment, insecurity, lack of trust and anger into adulthood—and into their own marriages.

Another way to look at it is that if there were a disease that affected more than 8 million people per year, it would be far more than a pandemic. It would be of epic proportions. Imagine if 8 million people a year contracted AIDS or the Swine Flu? The government would do everything it could to stem the tide of this disease and if possible find an antidote or any helpful hint to turn the corner. If people followed the same principles as the Menlo Park Singles, we might be able to turn the corner in epic proportions and give marriage a better chance.

Dating—The Danger of the Weird Zone

During the twentieth century, dating changed. It moved from a courtship in which society dictated the rules to a more independent form of interaction. People no longer relied on society or their parents to choose their spouses. With the rise of women's equality and increasing financial independence, more and more women had a greater voice in determining who they would date and who they would marry.[4] It meant that people could finally actually set up their own meetings with the opposite sex. This was a revolutionary change after the Victorian era. But that independence introduced a new problem.

When we find someone we like, something happens that makes dating exciting but confusing, allowing us to make very bad mistakes. A strange feeling comes over us when we start to like someone. It is called "The Crush"—or what I like to call "The Weird Zone."

Call it what you may, there comes a time when you start having romantic feelings for another and everything changes. You start obsessing over the person. You might get dizzy. Maybe you can't focus on anything but the person you like. The whole world seems happy, and you can become delirious with joy.

I love the movie scene in *(500) Days of Summer* when the main character, Tom, becomes so infatuated with Summer, the girl of his dreams, that he imagines that everyone who passes him is smiling and giving him high fives. People in the busy street start dancing with him in synchrony, joining him in his mirth, as even the UCLA marching band appears! (I was a student at the USC film school. If they had chosen the USC band, the film would probably have won an Oscar.)

What happens when you enter The Weird Zone? You can become infatuated, which means you start to *lose touch with reality*. Here are some signs that you have entered The Weird Zone:

- You no longer see any faults in the person;
- You want to spend every free moment with that person;
- You start trying to cut corners at work to be with that person;

• You stop listening to your friends' warnings about that person.

If you notice this in yourself or others, *be careful,* for you are entering The Weird Zone of infatuation. The irony is that you may be thinking, as you read this, *I don't want to follow these principles now. Don't need to.* But consider that maybe infatuation is blinding you from seeing the practicality of these truths.

It's at this critical time that the principles in the next chapter *must* be followed—or else The Weird Zone might lead you into a disastrous relationship.

Study Questions

1. When you consider the statistics and the crash-and-burn element of so many marriages, do you think it's possible to learn how to avoid divorce?

   _____

   _____

   _____

2. Have you or your family been affected by divorce personally? How does that event still impact your daily decisions and how you relate to other people?

   _____

   _____

   _____

3. Describe The Weird Zone from personal experience. What were you like in the Zone, and how did you see your romantic other? What was your view of the relationship after you left the Zone?

   _____

   _____

   _____

4. How long did being in The Weird Zone last? How did that time affect other areas of your life—work, school, non-romantic friendships?

   _____

   _____

   _____

5. The Weird Zone is always waiting in the wings when you are attracted to someone. Can you think of anything that would help a person make better decisions about dating? How would you approach getting into the Zone differently today?

   _____

   _____

   _____

Notes
1. The Barna Group, "New Marriage and Divorce Statistics Released."
2. Matthew D. Bramlett, William D. Mosher, "First Marriage Dissolution, Divorce and Remarriage, United States," Division of Vital Statstics, May, 31, 2001.
3. Email correspondence from Feldhahn, July 15, 2013.
4. Stephanie Coontz, *Marriage, A History: How Love Conquered Marriage* (New York: Penguin Books, 2005).

It Takes a Village to Choose a Spouse

Fools think their own way is right, but the wise listen to advice.

PROVERBS 12:15

Let's go back to that plane with the 20 to 39 percent chance of crashing and burning. Ask yourself again, *Would I get on that plane? Would I endanger my family or myself by getting on that plane?* Most of us would conclude that we would never get on that plane with such bad odds. Yet, we now know that getting married can be very precarious, especially if we lose our sense of reality and walk into The Weird Zone. I'd like to suggest principles you can follow to help clear your mind so that you can determine if the person you are dating might be the right spouse for you.

FIRST PRINCIPLE

You Need to Give Your Friends Permission to Honestly Speak into Your Life

Wounds from a sincere friend are better than
many kisses from an enemy (Proverbs 27:6, *NLT*).

We need to give permission to our friends to tell us the brutal facts about what they think of our date/boyfriend/girlfriend, because *it takes a village to choose a spouse.*

In this post-Victorian age, many do not have parents to help them choose a spouse. They do not have chaperones during a date to make sure the guy treats the girl right or the girl doesn't get too flirty. And while this may give us more freedom, we need to put safeguards in place to keep the right perspective. We have to compensate for the lack of extra perspective from parents and chaperones by having *someone* in our community who can speak the truth in love to us.

Right now you might be saying, "Aw, I don't need others to help me know if I have fallen in love with the right person." (Yeah, and notice the phrase "fall in love.") Our romantic feelings are like falling off a cliff without any control, leaving us to the blowing of the winds. We are just free falling, flailing our arms, out of control. "I can't help it," we cry. "I am just falling in love." Reasoning is now on the shelf. Feelings rule. We say we "just know it in our hearts" that this guy or this girl is the right one. *While that may be true for a great many people who have had successful marriages—that they just felt it was right—you need to know that the same percentage of the people who got divorced said a similar thing.*

So what made the difference? The difference is in friends who can warn us, inform us, show us and tell us about the faults of the person we are moving toward. "But," you say, "I *always* ask my friends to tell me what they think of my boyfriend (girlfriend)." Do you really? Or have you lied to yourself?

Here's how it normally goes. You say:

Hey, so Ryan and I have been dating for a while. Isn't he great? I just love his smile. He is so thoughtful. He always listens to me, and he knows my needs more than anyone else. And he is so close to God. And he prays all the time. He always thinks of others. I just think he is wonderful. He fills me with joy. I think he might be the one. So what do you think about Ryan?

At that point, no friend in his or her right mind would tell you what he or she *truly* thought about the person. You've painted your friend into a corner. Read the following question and look through the options, and you'll see what I'm talking about.

Exercise

Why does a friend *not* tell you what he or she thinks about your new beau, Ryan?

   a. Your friend doesn't want to hurt your feelings.

   b. Your friend doesn't want to hurt Ryan's feelings.

   c. Your friend doesn't want his or her feelings—or physical well-being—hurt by Ryan when he finds out what you said.

   d. Your friend doesn't want to burn bridges with you or Ryan in case you two get married.

   e. All of the above.

Yes, the answer is *E*—all of the above!

Somehow you have to . . . you simply must . . . I'm telling you it's mandatory—*give permission to your friends* to warn you if there are some bad things they perceive going on (or could go on) in your dating relationship. No friend wants to hurt you. She wants the best for you. He wants you to be happy. But you have to help him or her help you. Your friends know you. Allow them to get you out of The Weird Zone by encouraging them to speak honestly.

I was having lunch with friends in a famous Hollywood restaurant, and my friend said, "Hey, the last time I was here I saw [and she mentioned the name of a movie director] with his entourage and a beautiful blonde. They kept kissing each other in that booth over there."

"But isn't he married?" I asked.

"Yeah, and it's really hurting his wife," my friend said. "But, you know, he's a famous director. He's in The No Veto Zone. No one can tell him what to do—whether it's in his films, how he deals with people or, in this case, having an extramarital affair. Who can veto him? He's successful."

The worst thing you can do is put yourself in The No Veto Zone. And you are in big danger if you do not have friends who can make sure you don't go there. Find a friend, a pastor, a counselor, a parent or someone else you trust who can pull you out of The No Veto Zone—especially when you've wandered into The Weird

Zone—so that you can have more eyes and clearer vision. Being a frequent flyer in The Weird Zone *and* The No Veto Zone almost guarantees a crash and burn.

When you have friends who can talk to you honestly, it's like having friends in the control tower to guide you through a dark stormy night. Your plane's instruments are critical to your safety, but it's always better to land and take off with a control tower. The more friends you have who can talk to you honestly, the better your landing will be. Friends are your control tower.

More Eyes, Clearer Vision

Never get married in the morning, because you
never know who you'll meet that night.
Paul Hornung, former Green Bay Packers football player

There is a phrase that says, "*more eyes, clearer vision.*" In this case it means that the more people you have looking at your possible or present date, the better chance you will get an accurate read. We all see different facets of life. As the proverbial Elephant Story warns, if one only sees the trunk or the ear or the foot of the elephant, you don't have the full picture of the animal. Only when everyone contributes and reports what they see, do you see that it is an elephant.

When you are in the Weird Zone, you only see the trunk or the foot or the tusk or a toenail! You won't be able to see the faults of the other person—or even your own shortcomings—that might make your relationship combustible instead of harmonious for life. When you are infatuated, your radar couldn't ping an elephant if it were 10 feet from you; but your friend's radar is doing fine.

Listen carefully to what your trusted friends are trying to say to you. Yes, they could be wrong, but they are often right or at least in the ballpark.

Sometimes your friends will start off slowly to spare your feelings. Here's what I mean.

Exercise

Have you ever heard a friend say any of the following statements, or something similar, when speaking of your boyfriend or girlfriend?

  a. He's not the brightest crayon in the box.
  b. She's not playing with a full deck.
  c. Jesus loves him, but I'm not sure who else does.
  d. He is one taco short of a combination.
  e. I am not sure if his elevator goes to the top floor.
  f. He has one wheel stuck in the sand.
  g. How do you spell "sociopath"?

Humor can make it easier for a friend to sound a needed warning when the person you are falling in love with may not be the best choice for you.

Here is a recipe for disaster: A couple is about to make a commitment to be together for life; yet, all of their friends think it is a terrible mistake but say nothing. I know of someone who dated her boyfriend for 10 years and then, when they broke up, all of her friends said, "I didn't think he was good for you." They never said anything because they didn't think their friend wanted to hear their thoughts. Ten years lost to the wrong guy!

In fact, I have found that when a couple is about to make a very bad mistake in committing to be together for life, *almost always, all* of their friends also thought it was a mistake—but they never felt they could say anything. It's sad and tragic, but so avoidable if you will give trusted friends permission to speak honestly when they see something that raises a red flag about your dating relationship. If not, the pandemic of divorce will continue.

Designated Truth-Teller

When marrying, ask yourself: Do you believe that you will be able to converse well with this person into your old age? Everything else in marriage is transitory.
Friedrich Nietzsche

When people drink too much at a party, there is supposed to be a sober designated driver to get the inebriated partygoers home. All relationships need a designated truth-teller who can potentially keep a friend from getting stuck in a bad relationship. This is especially helpful when you are drunk with infatuation. The designated truth-teller asks you the hard questions. He or she shows you and your romantic partner in your real light.

Exercise

My designated truth-teller is:

1. A friend named _____
2. A pastor named_____
3. My parent _____
4. My relative _____
5. My therapist _____
6. Oh no, I don't have anyone!

Now, it's not fair to answer the above by saying, "Oh, I just tell God, and that is enough." That's a good thing to do, but it's not enough. The problem comes when a person thinks a boyfriend or girlfriend walks on water and has no faults. (Yeah, right!)

Remember, God often uses people here on earth to give a prophetic word of blessing or warning. In the Old Testament, Nathan the prophet warned David of impending doom because David had ordered his faithful soldier Uriah killed in order to marry Uriah's wife, Bathsheba (see 2 Samuel 12:9-12). Likewise, John the Baptist called out King Herod on his adultery (see Matthew 14:4). Joseph met Pharaoh and gave the frank, straight talk of a coming famine (see Genesis 41:25-36). It was Daniel who explained to King Belshazzar that the handwriting on the wall meant, "You have been weighed on the scales and found wanting" (Daniel 5:27).

Who is the person in your life who can read you the handwriting on the wall? Who would you let honestly say to you at a critical juncture in your life that you have been weighed and found wanting? Who can warn you that the person you are about to get more romantically interested in is the wrong guy or gal?

It is good to identify who those people are. But hear this: You need to set it up ahead of time or else such honesty can put you and your friends at odds with each other. At the very least, it will cause awkwardness. Give permission to your friends to speak into your life, and do it soon. It may mean that you need to practice today giving permission with other topics: Say, what do you think of this job I am considering? . . . this car I am buying? . . . this school I am thinking of attending? Practicing a lifestyle of giving people permission to speak honestly to you is healthy. If you haven't been in the practice of allowing people to speak into your life on lesser topics, it will be difficult to give them permission to speak on the choice of your spouse.

As I look back at my divorce, I can now recall that people tried to warn me that I was making a bad choice. I didn't listen. Some were pretty bold in trying to wave me off of a bad decision, but I was in The Weird Zone and I was unaccustomed to letting people speak truth into my life because I was basically naive.

In addition to having a lifestyle of giving permission to people to speak truth into our lives, we also need a lifestyle of receiving advice when given. We need to cultivate the humility to admit that we don't have all the answers and we don't see all the parts of the elephant in the room.

How did the singles of Menlo Park navigate the whole area of giving permission and receiving advice? They found a formal way to deal with it. The singles asked a pastor or therapist to intervene. The counselor or minister would observe and then speak to how the couple communicated and describe their chances for having a successful marriage, and why. But the singles did not rely only on professionals; they met regularly in small groups of 4 to 15 people. Meeting in small groups was a core value of the Menlo Park ministry. The singles met in their small groups on weekdays and also every Sunday night (for the young adults) after I taught.

Because of the small groups and the counsel of therapists and pastors, there was a greater chance for the community to speak into one another's lives. I regularly and consistently encouraged them to be open, vulnerable and transparent in those small groups.

Earlier, I said it takes a village to choose a spouse, but a "village" does not have to be very large. It might just be two or three people. But you need to listen to them. And if things are ever getting romantically serious, I highly recommend premarital counseling.

The Importance of Premarital Counseling

All one's ways may be pure in one's own eyes, but the Lord weighs the spirit (Proverbs 16:2).

In addition to giving your friends permission to be persons of truth with you, another useful safeguard is to go through premarital counseling. For the singles of Menlo Park, there was always the opportunity to go through premarital counseling. They did not have to wait for their engagement, which sometimes is too late to benefit from the counsel. But even in an engagement, it is never too late to pull back from a mistake.

To this day, as a pastor, I normally have three sessions with the couples I marry. In the Menlo Park days, as well as today, I would have the couple take tests—the Myers-Briggs Type Indicator (a personality test, also called Keirsey-Bates Temperament Sorter); the Edwards Personal Preference Schedule, which consists of 225 paired statements that show the relative importance to the individual of several significant needs and motives; plus a questionnaire I designed (see Appendix B). I'll talk more about these counseling tools in chapter 6.

Briefly, I used the questionnaire because it gave me insight from their self-disclosed data to talk about issues that might crop up in their dating style, background or culture. My first session with a couple was usually the toughest. At that session, I was trying to see whether (1) they were infatuated, (2) they had a realistic view of one another, or (3) there were some things in character or background that would be too hard to overcome. I would try to shake them up a bit to see if they had the right stuff to stay in a marriage. After putting them through the wringer, sometimes I would have to say,

"I don't think you two should get married." Those were the hardest meetings. But it was worth it to save two people from heartache, emotional scarring, and damage to their future children.

A few years ago, a woman named Sally came up to me at a conference at which I was speaking, and said, "You probably don't remember me, but in our premarital counseling session, you told me that I should not marry the guy I was with. I was so sad. But I realized later that you were right, and we broke up. But now, right here, I want to introduce you to my husband of the last 15 years, and we have three kids. I want to thank you. I am so happy! The other guy would not have worked out."

People like Sally make it all worth it. There are a number of singles I can remember to whom I strongly suggested they not marry the person they were with. They listened and are happily married today. Had they married the other person, it would have been a disaster. Most people come to counseling with so many issues from the past. You really need a community to help detect them.

I know that it can be devastating to be told that you and your significant other should not get married. If you agree with the assessment, it can still be quite painful to end it. But always remember that even if there is an ended engagement or relationship, that's not the end. You can still find a fulfilling relationship—as so many others have.

One of the best ways to navigate the entire dating process is with the help of a small group. The counsel of a small group of people can help you sail through the Weird Zone, tell you when you need to end a relationship, and support you through a breakup.

The Support of Small Groups

Where there is strife, there is pride, but wisdom is found in those who take advice (Proverbs 13:10, *NIV*).

Our small groups were a core value of the Menlo Park singles ministry, so it was basically expected that all of the singles would try to meet in a small group of 4 to 15 people. In those groups, they would study the Bible, pray for one another, and speak honestly about the issues they were facing. One group jokingly called themselves SLOBS—which stood for Singles Lonely Only Bible Study. It was a name that showed a lot of humor and humility. And it also showed a lot of confidence that allowed them to poke fun at themselves.

These groups met not only for laughs and to study the Bible, but they were also a tool to help their members find healthy relationships and work on areas that needed growth. They provided an opportunity for good friends to speak into each other's lives. It's the iron-sharpening-iron principle (see Proverbs 27:17). The groups were a place where, besides studying the principles of following Jesus and the Christian life, they could honestly talk about their issues of dating, jobs, dreams, heartaches and hopes.

On Sunday nights, we had more than 300 young adults in the sanctuary. After worship and a talk on a Bible passage, they would break up into small groups right there in the sanctuary and in nearby classrooms and fellowship halls. And in those small groups, many people gave each other the permission—in a small, intimate group setting—to share honest thoughts on a number of personal issues. People could get loving feedback from people they trusted.

Community is so important. We can't do it alone in the Christian life. There are no lone rangers, or there shouldn't be.

When it comes to dating, it really does take a village to grow us up to make the right choices in romantic relationships. If you don't yet have a regular small group to meet with, find some friends and give them permission to speak into your life. This step is critical!

Let's encourage honesty among ourselves as a top priority. But if you are finding it difficult to let your friends honestly speak into your life, there is another principle that will help: Don't rush the relationship. Read on.

Study Questions

1. Have you given your friends permission to speak honestly to you about any of your life choices, including your dating relationship? If not, why not?

   _____

   _____

   _____

   _____

2. Describe a time when you needed honesty from a friend—it could be any issue—and you sought it. What did you learn from that experience?

   _____

   _____

   _____

3. What would you have to do to build a lifestyle that regularly allows friends to guide you in life decisions?

   _____

   _____

   _____

4. What is preventing you from doing this? (Be honest with yourself!)

   _____

   _____

   _____

5. If you're not yet meeting with a small group of friends on a regular basis, how hard would it be to get it started? What's on your schedule right now that is less important than meeting with a small group?

   _____

   _____

   _____

Take a Lap Around the Track

For everything there is a season,
and a time for every matter under heaven.

ECCLESIASTES 3:1

SECOND PRINCIPLE

Date for a Year Before Getting Married

Exercise

Which of the following objects below best represents what a good relationship is like?

a. Microwave
b. Instant cocoa
c. Crockpot
d. Downloaded software
e. Quick battery charge

The answer is C—the crockpot!

It takes time to find a good relationship that will last for a lifetime. But it also takes time for a relationship to marinate enough to be ready for marriage. The late psychologist Walter Trobisch said a couple should be able to "summer and winter" together before deciding to get married.[1] I would add, a couple should be able to "simmer and boil" together to test the sturdiness of the relationship.

When people buy a car, they usually get really specific: They ask the dealer about the miles per gallon and how the seats move, and does it come in a certain color with a moon roof, where the spare tire is located; they ask about the terms of the warranty and the payment structure and even how many cup holders there are. There's lots of analysis! Do we do that with a possible marriage candidate, asking candid and frank questions about his or her state for the future?

Let's look at an even more expensive item, like purchasing a house. When people are considering a house, they check out all kinds of things.

They might walk over to a faucet and turn it on to see the water pressure.

They might look for rust on the pipes to see if they have to replace or fix them.

They search for signs of mold or leaks in the roof.

They might check to see how much maintenance the yard will need and if there are a lot of weeds.

They read a due diligence report from the seller to see if there were any recent damages or evidence of termites or rat problems.

They check to see if it is a good area for schools.

They investigate to see if the neighborhood is a high-crime area.

They ask about whether the traffic is bad, and they seek out the closest entrances to the freeway.

They might even check the Web to see if there are any convicted sex offenders in the neighborhood.

Maybe they even look to see if there are good churches or temples nearby.

I dare say that many people take more time to buy a house (which they can sell in a few years) than they do to determine if the person they are marrying is the right one (which should be a decision for a lifetime). It's funny when you think about it.

If you're willing to put that much time into buying a new house or a car, why not thoroughly observe how a person lives, reacts and responds over a period of time? You are picking a spouse for a lifetime, not a car with a five-year warranty. It's important to see your significant other function through all the seasons of a year. Take a lap around the track with him or her and see your potential spouse in the summer, fall, winter and spring of their lives—literally and figuratively. Give it at least a year.

See him under the pressure of a work deadline. See her when she is tired and cranky. See him as he fails to do some things he said he would do. See her when she does not get along with her parents (it also gives you a chance to see what you really think about your potential in-laws!). See what he is like when he doesn't get his way; see what she is like when you have an argument with her or when hormones are pulsating.

Getting to know your potential spouse over at least a year's time gives you the opportunity to ask yourself some key questions. For instance: How does your potential partner reconcile conflict? Is he good at it? Does she get angry and unreasonable? Does he yell? Does she get really quiet or passive-aggressive? Can you live with his or her way of communicating?

After discovering the answers to these questions, ask yourself, *Can I handle that for a lifetime?*

Exercise

What is the best answer to the question below?

During an argument, it's okay if my partner:

    a. Always thinks he/she is right.
    b. Loses his/her temper.
    c. Hits me.
    d. Hits the wall.
    e. Pouts.
    f. Has a hard time saying, "I'm sorry."
    g. Storms out of the house.
    h. Throws things at me.

The answer: There is no best answer; these are all "red flag" behaviors.

Marriage Is Like Dating—Only More So

*For nothing is hidden that will not be disclosed,
nor is anything secret that will not become
known and come to light (Luke 8:17).*

So, you're getting to know your potential spouse over several seasons of life. What do your observations indicate for your marriage? If you observe a consistently positive set of behaviors, or behaviors you know you can live with, start making your wedding plans. But if you are having a hard time during courtship, *it only gets worse in marriage*.

Why is this the case? When people are dating, they are usually on their best behavior and will lie about their likes or dislikes in order to please the person with whom they are in The Weird Zone.

True story: A girlfriend says to her boyfriend, "I love opera. Will you go with me to the theater?" The guy hates opera. But he is trying to woo her, so he says, "Sure, I'll go with you, honey. I'll go whenever you want to." But when they get married, the guy is suddenly too tired or busy to go to the opera. He shocks her with the news that he hates opera. He thinks he doesn't need to try to sacrifice and impress her anymore. It could just as easily have been, "But you said you liked Country and Western music!"

Another true case study: The guy loves going to football games, watching the games on TV at home and sometimes going out later for some drinks with the guys. The girlfriend says, "I love football!" When they get married, she suddenly hates it when he is watching football on TV and wants him to turn it off during the playoffs, and not stay out so late and . . . oh, by the way, she says, "Superbowl and fantasy football are a waste of time!" Stunning news for the guy!

Sadly, this is a common scenario for couples who just don't know each other well enough. They haven't taken a lap around the track.

When people are courting, they usually get dressed up more. They check how their breath smells. They wash their hair and keep it combed. They wear their nicest clothes. They give gifts and cards more often. They express gratitude all the time. But talk to your friends who have been married a long time. You'll find that a lot of that changes in marriage.

So, if you are arguing a lot in your relationship while dating (while on your *best* behavior), it very often will only get worse after you are married. In fact, if people are arguing a lot during courtship, that means bad news for marriage. Sure, there can be bickering or grousing even in a good marriage; but there are certain arguments that are hurtful and will only get worse. It's a hard truth, but I've seen it time and again: Most people argue more in marriage than in courtship. So if you are already arguing a lot while dating, I would say, "*Sayonara, adios, aloha, auf Wiedersehen.*"

If there are a lot of arguments through the four seasons of the year, believe me, there are other people out there you should consider! He's not the right one. Save yourself the migraines. If she gets on your nerves now, she will really get on your nerves after you are married. Similarly, think of the small courtesies like saying "please" and "thank you." In marriage, those often disappear. So if you are not getting courtesy and pleasant conversation while you're dating, it is going to be much harder later.

I remember watching an elderly couple hitting golf balls on a driving range. They were so affirming to each other, even when one of them hit a bad shot. I said to my friend, "I bet they are dating, and not married." He said, "But they appear on the older side. They must be married. They seem to be in their seventies."

"No way," I said. "They are dating."

I went up to them to find the answer and said, "It is so nice to hear you encouraging one another. You must have been married a long time."

The man said, "Oh no, we just go out with each other. We're friends."

Unfortunately, when I see a couple in a restaurant staring intently at each other and truly trying to listen to one another, I think they must be dating. If I see the man pull out the chair for the woman to help seat her, I really know they are dating!

Many of the common courtesies demonstrated during courtship, like opening doors and pulling out chairs and truly listening to one another, fall by the wayside in marriage. That's why it's important to take note, while dating, of how the person handles ups and downs. And if you don't even have good communication and common courtesies while dating, then that person is not the one for you.

There has to be at least a basic healthy starting point. If you see rudeness, lack of common decency, a lot of arguing, poor communication, misunderstanding and lack of trust while dating, then believe me, there are other fish in the ocean, and you should go fish for someone else.

In taking that lap around the track, it will also make all the difference in the world if you have a clear picture of who *you* are. If you put up with a lot of arguing and conflict, then maybe you should get counseling and find the reason why you do that. Is there something in your past that keeps you from seeing when a relationship is toxic? That keeps you tolerating hurtful talk and harmful behavior?

When I do premarital counseling, it is not unusual to hear a couple say things like, "I have finally found someone who accepts me as I am and who really understands me." Yet, I often hear married couples say, "She is always trying to change me," or "I hate it when he keeps doing [fill in the behavior] again and again. Sometimes I really don't understand him." Statements like these mean that what couples saw in courtship was not the real thing. They based their dating on fiction, not fact. When you take a lap around the track, wintering and summering with someone, you will get a better chance of seeing the real person and shortening the gap between infatuation and reality.

It's a fact that (and I'm sorry if I'm about to hurt your feelings here) you are a sinner and so is your partner. *The reason why marriage is so hard is that a marriage partner is the one person on earth who sees more fully the sinful nature of his or her spouse, and vice versa. Do we have the skills to deal with that?* Our human nature has a selfish core. We are often self-serving and self-centered. You have heard the phrase "trophy children" or "trophy spouse"; part of our motivation in getting married or having children is to enjoy an *extension* of self. We enjoy looking good by having that handsome guy or that cute girl by our side. But don't forget that the handsome guy or cute girl is a sinner just like you with plenty of faults you have yet to discover and learn to accept if you choose to marry him or her.

When you put your fiancé(e), girlfriend or boyfriend in a position where he or she is the only one who makes you feel complete or is the only one who understands you, then you are putting that person on a throne where only God should sit. It is a subtle thing, but I think couples often get divorced because they unknowingly put their spouse in the place of God. Only God can truly fill your needs. Only God can truly forgive you and give you the meaning and guidance you want. God can work through your spouse, but your spouse is not God. The more you put your spouse in God's place, the more you are in la-la land, and still living in The Weird Zone.

A strong physical connection can make that Weirdness even more intense and difficult to break through. As you will see in the next chapter, physical chemistry is important, but you need to fully understand the natural dynamics of a sexual relationship. Otherwise, you'll be flying blind in The Weird Zone.

Study Questions

1. Have you known any microwave marriages? How have they differed from crockpot marriages?

   _____

   _____

   _____

2. How does the thought of a year of courtship strike you? Does it seem practical? Do you have any resistance to this exhortation? Why?

   _____

   _____

   _____

3. Why do you think people are on their best behavior when dating? Why might that cease (or greatly decrease) during marriage?

_____

_____

_____

4. What could you do to make sure that doesn't happen to you?

_____

_____

_____

5. Have you hidden any behaviors when dating? Would any of those hidden behaviors threaten a future marriage? If so, would you seriously consider investing time in counseling about it? If not, why not?

_____

_____

_____

Note

1. Walter Trobisch, *I Married You* (Bolivar, MO: Quiet Waters Publications, 2009).

Sex Before Marriage

*It is easier to suppress the first desire than
to satisfy all that follows it.*

BENJAMIN FRANKLIN

In Choosing a Spouse, It's in Your Best Interests to Not Have Sex Before Marriage

After reading that third principle, you might like to say to me, "Of course you would say that! You are a pastor, so of course you would say that sex before marriage is against God's will!" While that may be true, I actually have many more reasons to say it *apart* from a Christian faith perspective. Whenever I talk about premarital sex, I always start from the purely practical, street-savvy aspect of building a healthy dating relationship. Only after that do I get into faith reasons for waiting to have sex.

The secular counterargument would be, "You gotta kick the tires to check the air pressure." This means, if you're going to marry this person, and sex is an important part of any marriage, then you'd better test how sexually compatible you are with your romantic other. You need to take her for a test drive. You need to see if you and he can communicate in the sexual arena, because it is such a critical part of marriage.

While this all seems reasonable and logical, this is not the helpful state of mind and action plan you might imagine. In truth, having sex before marriage can make it *more difficult* to find the right person for a successful marriage.

Binds and Blinds

When you have sex with someone, it binds you to that person. You feel an emotional and spiritual connection. Sex is a physical, volitional, emotional experience. All of our body and soul is involved in having sex. Yes, it feels good. Yes, it is pleasurable. But the danger of sex before marriage is that it binds you emotionally to a person way before you really know the person and way before your mind is ready for a commitment. To me, it's like physically engaging in a relationship with "eyes wide shut" (to use the title of a Stanley Kubrick film).

You feel connected to the other person in more ways than one. Sex makes you think, *prematurely,* that he (or she) is the one. The physical satisfaction may trick you into thinking that you have found the woman (the man) you have always wanted—even if this is not necessarily true in other important areas. Sex can increase infatuation at a time when you desperately need to look at a person's personality in a seriously realistic way.

Part of the reason a person feels so bound to the one with whom he or she is having a romantic encounter is that a hormone called oxytocin is released in the body that emotionally binds you to the other person. It is the same hormone secreted when a baby is nursing and that creates such an emotional bond between mother and child.

While you may think it is because of *love* that you are so attract-ed to the person with whom you are having sex, that feeling is also due to the oxytocin. The surge of the hormone can actually weaken or overcome objective thoughts. You may become more emotionally bonded way before your commitment to the other person has had a chance to develop.

Sex before marriage can also blind you to a person's faults—faults that are so great that they are actually hazardous to the health of a marriage. When you have sex, you want it again and again. You begin to spend more time making out, having sex or pursuing it, and less time on the important things you need to build up—your intellec-tual, spiritual, emotional and communicative compatibility. In fact, conversation can fall completely by the wayside.

In the Bible, in the book of Genesis, we are told that in a mar-riage union the man must leave his father and mother and *cleave* to his wife and they shall become *one* flesh (see Genesis 2:24). That cleaving is such a strong union that it is like two pieces of paper getting glued to one another. They become one. That is why divorce is so painful: You can't separate two pieces of glued paper without tearing them—separation makes them rip apart. Divorce is a tearing of the heart and soul. Even when a relationship has grown stale, trying to separate two people's love for one another turns into a ripping of the soul.

Cleaving is a commitment that should only be made after you have taken the time needed to see if that person is the one you can spend the rest of your life with. Only when you have made an honest appraisal of whether you and your love interest have the maturity to make a lifelong commitment to each other should you two become one flesh—meaning, have sex. And that should happen only after a public ceremony before your village of friends and family, declaring your forever love for one another—that is, a wedding. Words alone are cheap; the *public commitment* and sharing of vows are critical to the success of the relationship, along with the approval of friends/pastors/small-group members.

Sex means that you become one flesh. Whenever you have sex with a person, a part of your heart goes with that person. If you have multiple sexual experiences, then you have become emotionally bonded with a number of people and with all of the memories—both good and bad. It is not God's intention for our hearts to have that many intimate relationships with people other than our spouse.

Sex is always safest in the context of marriage—but first you need to determine if that person is the right spouse material by delaying sex. Only in the context of complete trust and commitment can sex be experienced to its fullest. Another reason to avoid sex before marriage is to avoid unwanted pregnancy and disease.

Unwanted Pregnancy

I wish I was one of those cute pregnant
girls who wear skinny jeans throughout their
pregnancies. But I just gain weight.
Jennifer Garner, actress

If you have sex before marriage, you have greatly increased the chances of having an unwanted pregnancy. And if you get pregnant while unmarried, you will be forced into some really tough decisions: You are forced to decide whether you need to get married before you are really ready to make a commitment; or you have to put up a child for adoption or become a single parent when you aren't ready; or you may even have an abortion, which the Bible teaches is the taking of a life that God created in its mother's womb (see Psalm 139:13).

This chapter is not about whether or not you should have an abortion. It is about whether you even want to risk getting pregnant by choosing to have sex outside of marriage. Besides, there are more dangers in premarital sex than pregnancy.

Disease

> What sense would it make or what would it benefit a physician if he discovered the origin of the diseases but could not cure or alleviate them?
> Paracelsus (sixteenth-century toxicologist, who coined the words "zinc," "gas," "chemistry," "alcohol")

When you have sex with someone who has had sex with others, you are having sex with the *entire history* of that person's sexual partners. And if he or she had sex with someone who had a disease, that history becomes part of your history.

Do you know what genital human papillomavirus (HPV) is? According to the Centers for Disease Control and Prevention (CDC), it is the most common sexually transmitted infection (STI). There are more than 40 types of HPV. To quote the CDC:

> Anyone who is having (or has ever had) sex can get HPV. HPV is so common that nearly all sexually active men and women get it at some point in their life. . . . HPV is passed on through genital contact, most often during vaginal and anal sex. HPV may also be passed on during oral

sex and genital-to-genital contact. HPV can be passed on between straight and same-sex partners—even when the infected person has no signs or symptoms. Most infected persons do not realize they are infected or that they are passing HPV on to a sex partner. A person can still have HPV, even if years have passed since he or she has had sexual contact with an infected person. It is also possible to get more than one type of HPV. Most people with HPV never develop symptoms or health problems. Most HPV infections (90%) go away by themselves within two years. But, sometimes HPV infections will persist and can cause a variety of serious health problems.[1]

These problems include warts on the genital area and throat; cervical cancer; head and neck cancer, including the base of the tongue and tonsils; cancer of the penis and anus. If one chooses to sleep around, know that approximately 79 million Americans are currently infected with HPV, with about 14 million more people newly infected every year. Pregnant women can get infected with HPV and in rare cases can pass it on to their children, causing respiratory illness. Condoms may not protect you from HPV. Vaccines are available for children starting from age 11 up through adults of 26 years of age to prevent HPV.[2]

HPV is nothing compared to gonorrhea, a painful disease that is becoming resistant or immune to medicine that was used to treat it in the past. The World Health Organization estimates that about 62 million people a year get gonorrhea due to contact with the mouth, penis, vagina or anus of an infected sexual partner.[3] It can spread to the uterus and fallopian tubes, which increases the risk of pelvic inflammatory disease, the inability to have babies, and ectopic pregnancy—a medical condition that can be a life-threatening when an embryo gets implanted outside the uterus.

Gonorrhea can also be passed on from mother to child, so it goes on to the next generation and increases the risk of HIV. Obviously, sexually transmitted diseases can be harmful, dangerous and painful for guys in their genital area. As I already mentioned, gonorrhea is no longer responsive to penicillin. By 2010,

27 percent of all gonorrhea tested was found to be *resistant* to three major antibiotics or some combination of them. In 2011, the Centers for Disease Control estimated that close to 700,000 people had gonorrhea in the U.S. alone.[4]

The future of sexually transmitted disease does not look good. Every year millions of new people in the U.S. are getting a sexually transmitted disease. What to do? You can hope for new drugs to be invented or—here is a novel idea—refrain from having sex outside of marriage.

If you have sex before marriage, you risk these occurrences:

- a. Disease
- b. Death
- c. Pain
- d. Unwanted pregnancy
- e. Abortion
- f. Infertility
- g. Being bound emotionally and prematurely to an incompatible partner
- h. Being blinded to a person's faults
- i. Living against God's will

Or . . . you can follow God's plan for sex and reserve it until you can enjoy it within the commitment of marriage.

While some people say you should examine the relationship by taking that test-drive and having sex with the person, the true answer is that if you perceive that a person is sensitive and caring in communication with you—then you probably have enough evidence that you won't need to experiment with sex before marriage. A caring person who can communicate with you will likely translate to a sensitive and caring sexual partner. And when you give yourself in marriage to a caring person who is gentle and thoughtful and trustworthy, who has your interests at heart, you will experience the best sex in the world.

However, if you have sex too early in the relationship, you might become blinded to recognizing if that person is truly caring and sensitive.

Everyone's Doing It!

The character Barney Stinson, in the TV show *How I Met Your Mother*, claims he has slept with a minimum of 200 women. Normally, we would think this guy is a sex addict, but he is seen as a likable character on the show. The main character, Ted Mosby, has slept with one of the main characters, Robin Scherbatsky, who has also slept with Barney. In one show, Robin is living with another man who discovers that Robin has slept with half her friends. This all is seen as *normal!* The implication is that you can have sex with anyone and it doesn't affect friendship.

This is seen also in the TV show *Seinfeld* where Jerry and Elaine had sex together but then went on as friends as if nothing happened. In real life, it isn't as if nothing happened. Do you know any friendships like that? I don't. I believe a piece of your heart goes with everyone you have had sex with and it does take an emotional toll. As I said earlier, it creates a bond that is not necessarily healthy.

Conor Friedersdorf's article in *Atlantic* magazine, entitled "Young People Who Sacrifice Romance for 'Unencumbered Striving',￼" reports that the "hookup culture" is not just driven by young men. Women see it as a "functional strategy for today's hard-charging and ambitious young women, allowing them to have enjoyable sex lives while focusing most of their energy on academic and professional goals."[5] So the thinking is that because there is no time for romantic involvements that might lead to marriage, just have no-strings hookups with guys. Then, maybe when you are 28 or 30, you can get married. But the article asks the question: How do you make that shift from "no-strings" to dating to marriage without any major psychological, emotional problems? For many, sex outside of marriage is seen as having no emotional repercussions. It is a tool merely for pleasure. What a lie!

Unfortunately, I think that society takes a lot of its cues for behavior from Hollywood filmmakers who help create the belief that everyone is having premarital sex or affairs without consequences. Hollywood says, in essence, "Everyone is doing it." But to make matters worse, TV-Movie Land implies that everyone is doing it outside of marriage! Did you ever notice that in all of the hundreds of thousands of movies made, *you rarely see married people have sex?*

The sex we see on the screen is premarital or extramarital, not marital sex.

Try this test; you have one minute.

Exercise

List 10 movies that show a married couple having pleasurable, passionate sex.

1. _____
2. _____
3. _____
4. _____
5. _____
6. _____
7. _____
8. _____
9. _____
10. _____

Did you even come up with five movie titles? Hollywood says that real, passionate, pleasurable sex happens outside of marriage; so have sex outside of marriage. That's where the real fun is.

We're being brainwashed and bombarded with thousands and thousands of films depicting sex this way, and it seeps into our souls as normal behavior! That is so far from the truth—the best sex happens within the safety of a lifelong commitment of marriage. It is in the context of marital vows that you and your body can feel fully accepted; where you can be creative and experiment and experience different ways of finding pleasure without feeling you would be rejected. God designed the best performance and enjoyment of sex to happen within marriage.

How Much Is a Virgin Worth?

CNN.com and the *Telegraph* in the United Kingdom reported that in September 2009, 22-year-old Natalie Dylan of San Diego, California, made a bold decision. She heard that her sister made a lot of money as a prostitute to pay for her college degree. Ms. Dylan decided she also wanted to sell her body to make money for her master's degree in Marriage and Family Therapy (she already had a degree in Women's Studies). But she took a different track from her sister's. She decided to go on the Internet and sell her virginity to the highest bidder. She offered her virginity at an auction through the Moonlite Bunny Ranch, a legal brothel in Nevada.

Exercise

How high did the bid go for Natalie Dylan's virginity?

1. $10
2. $150
3. $1,000
4. $100,000
5. $1 million
6. $3.7 million

The answer is *E*, $3.7 million!

Ten thousand men bid for her offer on the Internet,[6] which indicates that our society greatly values virginity. Both the world and Christianity affirm and value virginity. So don't throw yours away too early.

If you are a virgin, keep your virginity for the person you know you want to spend the rest of your life with. If you are reading this and you are not a virgin, then strive to be one from here on. Know that God's forgiveness is real and that from here on you can write a new chapter on how your future relationships will be conducted. God's forgiveness, grace and mercy not only clean our slate but also throw away the slate so that we can start anew with His wisdom and blessings.

How important is it to accept the forgiveness and inner healing God alone offers? It should be of highest importance! God's grace and unconditional love for us are so great—beyond our wildest imagining—as you can see in this true story.

I have spoken nationally and internationally at conferences on the importance of wisely choosing a spouse. After one of these conferences, I received an email from a woman named Jenny. She wrote that when she heard me talk about the importance of virginity she felt "a crashing sadness." Here is what she said:

> Being raised in the Bible Belt to a conservative Christian family, I was raised to believe in abstinence. I even organized and led the "True Love Waits" rallies in my high school, where everyone was emotionally manipulated to sign a pledge card. LOL. This is all really great, and I'm glad it helped me as long as it did as a young woman, but by putting the emphasis on staying a virgin as a key component to what it means to follow Jesus and to be a Christian, I was setting myself up for a complete faith crisis later in life. My self-worth and faith was [sic] built in the list of do's and don'ts that were easy to keep . . . for a while. . . .
>
> As I heard about the virginity auction in your talk, I heard a voice in my mind that always creeps into these conversations that says, "You are worth nothing now. You are repulsive; no godly man will ever want you." And, "You are worthless to God's kingdom." While people from my background know the value of virginity, we still don't know the value of self.
>
> Well, praise God, I know the voice of the Good Shepherd, and He quickly said in my spirit, "NOOO, JENNY, you are worth far more than $3.7 million; I GAVE MY LIFE FOR YOU. I took your shame."
>
> The thing is, those men don't value the woman you spoke of who auctioned off her body. They won't value her like a good spouse will. They wanted to violate and use her for their sick fantasy of being with a virgin. Praise God my future husband won't base my worth on that.
>
> So, I would say there is forgiveness and a new start for those who have not waited. Being a good partner will require me to know my value and to have it completely centered, as you say in your talks, on the truth.

I know your talk was not a "self-worth and inner healing" speech, but not all of your listeners may have the weapon I have to hear Jesus telling them the truth, and they may get discouraged and just quit trying.

P.S. A side note and personal story: In one of my darkest hours, years ago, I stood in the shower feeling so much shame. I wrote in the mist on the shower door the word "whore" and I just cried. The memory of that pain stuck with me a long while. I felt like I wanted to run the race with God but was doing it with a bum leg . . . shame.

One night, I literally had a dream that I was back in that same shower. Everything was the same! Except Jesus was actually standing in the shower with me. He showed me His hands and pointed to the water going down the drain. Then, in my dream, He took His hand and wiped away the word "whore" I had written in the mist and wrote "Beloved." When I woke up from that dream, I felt free. I still feel free every time I tell it. My life's calling is to help people feel the freedom Jesus has given us! YAY!!![7]

Jenny ended her email with two Bible verses:

For the accuser of our brothers, who accuses them before our God day and night, has been hurled down. They overcame him by the blood of the Lamb and by the word of their testimony (Revelation 12:10-11).

Jesus straightened up and asked her [a woman caught in the act of adultery who was about to be stoned], "Woman, where are they? Has no one condemned you?" "No one sir," she said. "Then neither do I condemn you," Jesus declared. "Go now and leave your life of sin" (John 8:10-11).

I would add to Jenny's poignant email the next verse in the Gospel of John: "Again Jesus spoke to them, saying, 'I am the light of the world. Whoever follows me will never walk in darkness but will have the light of life'" (John 8:12).

God's Will

"For this is the will of God . . ." (1 Thessalonians 4:3).

I said I would wait until the end to give you the religious answer about sex before marriage, from a pastor's perspective. You might be surprised that I waited this long. But I wanted to make the case that, even apart from a biblical perspective, there are a lot of good reasons to wait to have sex within marriage, including the fact that it will be the safest place and it will also enhance your odds in choosing the right person.

People always say, "I would love to know God's will for my life. If I knew it, I would just do it." Well, twice in the Bible it actually says, "This is the will of God." Can't be any plainer than that. God says, do this!

One passage tells us to "Rejoice always, pray without ceasing, give thanks in all circumstances; for this is the will of God in Christ Jesus for you" (1 Thessalonians 5:16-18). That's a good verse. God desires us to always be joyous, prayerful, thankful people. There aren't many people who would object to those verses. That kind of attitude in life brings a lot of benefits.

The second Scripture is also pretty clear and straightforward about what God thinks is best for us. It says, "For *this is the will of God*, your sanctification: that you abstain from fornication" (1 Thessalonians 4:3, emphasis added). There it is. *This is the will of God*, your sanctification—meaning that you are holy, aligned with God's destiny for your life. And how do you participate in the will of God? By abstaining from fornication. The word "fornication" comes from the Greek word *porneia,* which means sex outside of marriage—it's the same root from which we get the word "pornography." If you want to do the will of God, then abstain from sex outside of marriage. God doesn't give us much wiggle room on this one.

This is the will of God: to abstain from sex outside of marriage. Why? For all of the reasons we've just discussed: that you would have the best chance in choosing a spouse with your eyes open; that you wouldn't ever have to worry about getting an unwanted disease or pregnancy; so that you would be living a life according to how God designed our psyche and our bodies to function best. Just as a car maker gives us a manual of how our car runs best, God, the human maker, has given us the Bible to tell us how to live our lives in optimum fashion—even though it may seem counterintuitive to all that we hear from the media.

God Is for Excellence

God's will for your life is to live it in the most excellent way. He is into excellence. When we hear beautiful music, watch inspiring theater, admire an awesome mountain range or delight in the color of changing leaves in the fall, we see God's excellence.

Anything of worth is of God, and His excellence reigns. God is not only about excellence; He *is* excellence. And when God created us, He didn't create junk. He wants us to live the excellent way. And when it comes to our bodies, He designed sex, according to His will, to be done in the context of marriage. In marriage there should be safety—if there is a pregnancy, and safety in communicating to the one who is committed to you about what you like or may dislike in sex.

The physical expression of love should only grow as your knowledge and commitment to another person grows. Ideally, that growth should be parallel and in unison. It should look like this:

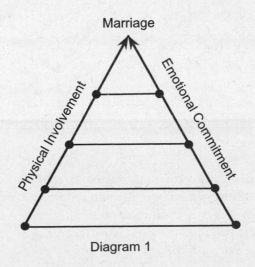

Diagram 1

As a couple grows in knowing each other and their physical communication moves toward physical intimacy, sexual intercourse should only happen at the pinnacle of their commitment—after the wedding, which declares publicly that the couple is truly committed to each other for the rest of their lives. Sex should only happen after there has been what Walter Trobisch calls "summering and wintering" together. This is so that the public declaration is a mature one based on time with and knowledge of one's mate. The goal is to do things at the same pace so that there is an equilateral triangle.

You don't want the physical involvement to go faster than the commitment of love or the diagram will look like this. Notice that the relationship between the physical and emotional commitment is no longer parallel; instead, it is off balance. The physical is way farther along than the stage of commitment of the relationship.

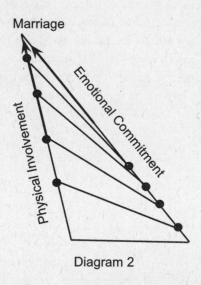

Diagram 2

Nor do you want the commitment to be so far ahead of the physical that it might cause rigidity and frigidity in marriage because there has never been any physical touch, like hand-holding or kissing. When this is the case, it all happens too quickly and that triangle would look like this:

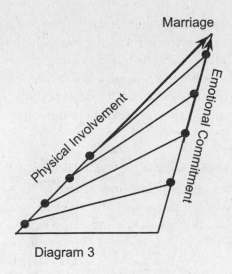

Diagram 3

In truth, romance is not easily balanced in a relationship. Like playing an instrument or scripting a play, everything of excellence is about timing, balance and pacing. It takes effort to get it right. Hence, the knowledge and experience of sex is more analogous to riding an escalator than an elevator. Let me show you what I mean.

Elevator vs. Escalator

Some people think sex is like going between floors in an elevator. You can get very physical and go to the tenth floor, but then very easily hit a button and go down to just hand-holding on the third floor. In reality, it is extremely difficult to go up and down from heavy petting to just hand-holding in a romantic relationship. When you go from hand-holding to kissing to petting, you have started a ride on which you will always want to escalate the physical intimacy until it peaks with sexual intercourse. That is why you should take your time with the physical part of your dating relationship. Getting to the equilateral triangle requires conscious effort on your part.

"But," you might be saying, "that takes all the fun out of it." It's not that romance shouldn't be fun. It's just that romance leads to one of the most important decisions in your life: choosing a mate. So there had better be some rationality in the physical romance area, or else you may choose unwisely. Divorce is very, very painful. It can be destructive and scarring to the soul. Choosing a mate is not like buying a car or a house that you can sell. It's not like a job that you can leave. This is about finding the lifelong mate who can truly bring much happiness and joy to your life.

The Myth of the Wisdom of Cohabitation

Our culture's take on choosing a mate is "You have to kick the tires and check the pressure." The idea that you need to live with someone to make sure he or she is the right one sounds practical, doesn't it? Well, it is not! It's *counterintuitive to the way God created us to thrive with a partner*. God says we shouldn't have sex before marriage, even if it seems crazy in the secular world's eyes. Here's the reality of what happens when we choose to cohabitate before marriage:

The Barna Group surveyed 5,017 people age 18 and older from January 2007 through 2008, and reported:

> Government statistics and a wealth of other research data have shown that cohabitation increases the likelihood of divorce, yet cohabitation is growing in popularity. Studies show the importance and value of preparing for marriages seem to fall on deaf ears. America has become an experimental, experience-driven culture. Rather than learn from objective information and teaching based on that information, people prefer to follow their instincts and let the chips fall where they may. Given that tendency, we can expect America to retain the highest divorce rate among all developed nations of the world.[8]

International scholar on family and marriage, and founder of the National Marriage Project, David Popenoe, wrote, "Many studies in the US have shown that couples who cohabit before marriage have a higher risk of divorce when they do marry."[9] Several reasons have been put forth to account for this. One is that it is mostly due to selectivity; that is, those people who are willing to cohabit are the same people who already are more divorce prone. They may be less committed to traditional family values, less inclined toward or more tentative regarding long-term relationships, and may have personality traits that make them less suitable as marriage partners.

A second reason involves the actual experience of cohabitation, that is, attitudes and behaviors developed through cohabitation may be inimical to long-term marriage. For example, cohabitation may generate the attitude that relationships are mainly for the purpose of testing compatibility, an attitude poisonous to long-term marriages.

A third reason is that cohabiting couples, compared to dating couples, often find it harder to break up due to the greater complications of household and financial as well as emotional matters. They therefore may drift through inertia into inappropriate marriages, only to break up farther down the line.[10]

More recently, the *Wall Street Journal* quoted sociologist Brad Wilcox giving a summary of a report for the RAND Corporation written by Michael Pollard and Kathleen Harris that stated, "Pollard and Harris found that the majority of cohabiting young men do not endorse the maximum indicator of relationship permanence: 52 percent of cohabiting men between ages 18 and 26 are not 'almost certain' that their relationship is permanent. Moreover, a large minority (41 percent) of men report that they are not 'completely committed' to their live-in girlfriends. By contrast, only 39 percent of cohabiting women in the same age group are not 'almost certain' their relationship will go the distance, and only 26 percent say they are not 'completely committed.'"[11]

You might be thinking, *Geez, not living together and not having sex seems so outdated and old-fashioned. The Bible is so narrow and out of it.* If you're thinking that, here's what you are really saying: *I am choosing to believe that my outlook and thinking today are absolute. I am perfect in how I perceive reality, and what the Bible is saying is irrelevant and not the truth. I have the truth in how I see things in my contemporary fashion.* The basic question is, where do you really put your trust—in the wisdom of God's Word, the Bible—or in your absolute contemporary beliefs? The problem with a person's absolute contemporary beliefs becomes apparent when a person tries to recall how he or she saw life, let's say, 10 years ago, or even how society saw truth 80 years ago. Contemporary beliefs are not so absolute!

You might be embarrassed to realize how what you used to think was truth is no longer truth to you. That is the danger of seeing how you view reality today as perfect versus how the Bible sees it—the same yesterday, today and tomorrow.

Just look at food groups. We thought eating mainly red meat and potatoes was the right way to diet. But then we learned over the decades that we were wrong—that, actually, certain food groups had too much fat and cholesterol or sugar, and we should eat more plant-based protein and fruits and leafy vegetables. We may have thought 20 years ago that fast food was really good to eat often, but that's not true. Think of the way we treated the environment decades ago; now we see that we might have been grossly wrong. Or, decades ago, we thought smoking was cool but then we learned it's a deadly health risk for cancer.

One final thing before we close this chapter. I want to make it clear that God is pro-sex. Sex is good. Sex is a gift. Sex is pleasurable. It is not bad. But God designed it to be expressed in a context of trust, loyalty and never-ending commitment. In a word: *marriage*.

Having sex is important. But let's be clear: It is a strong want, not a need. You need water, food, air, shelter. You can die without these needs being met. To this date, we do not know of anyone who has died due to a lack of sex. You might feel like you are dying, but you are not. It is a want, and it is a big want. But there are couples that can't have sex due to physical or emotional challenges; and yet they have a great, loving marriage.

Sex is important, but there are other elements in a marriage that might be more important than sex, and you *need* those things to make a marriage work. Those elements are what we will look at in the next chapter.

Study Questions

1. What would you say is the most compelling reason not to have sex before marriage?

   _____

   _____

   _____

   _____

2. What is your greatest objection to waiting until marriage to have sex?

   _____

   _____

   _____

   _____

3. What do you think of the author's view that sex before marriage creates emotional ties that cause pain and can scar the psyche?

   _____

   _____

   _____

   _____

4. How does our contemporary culture feed the lie about cohabitation as a smart thing to do?

   _____

   _____

   _____

   _____

5. What is the most compelling takeaway from this chapter for you about the wisdom of saving sex for marriage?

   _____

   _____

   _____

Notes
1. "Genital HPV Infection—Fact Sheet," Centers for Disease Control and Prevention, July 27, 2013. http://www.cdc.gov/std/hpv/stdfact-hpv.htm (accessed October 2013).
2. Ibid.
3. Anna Tomausulo, "Sex and the Superbug: Meet Antibiotic-Resistant Gonorrhea," *The Disease Daily*, a publication from HealthMap at Boston Children's Hospital, May 24, 2013.
4. Ibid.
5. Conor Friedersdorf, "Young People Who Sacrifice Romance for 'Unencumbered Striving,'" *Atlantic*, July 16, 2013, from a one-year study by Kate Taylor of 60 women at the University of Pennsylvania.
6. "Student Auctions Off Virginity for Offers of More Than £2.5 million," January 12, 2009. telegraph.uk.com (accessed October 2013).
7. Used by permission.
8. "New Marriage and Divorce Statistics," The Barna Group, March 31, 2008.
9. Binstock and Thorton, op.cit.; and Jay Teachman, "Premarital Sex, Premarital Co-habitation, and the Risk of Subsequent Marital Dissolution Among Women," *Journal of Marriage and Family* 65 (2003): 444-455; Claire M. Kamp Dush, C. L. Cohan and P. R. Amato, "The Relationship Between Cohabitation and Marital Quality and Stability: Change Across Cohorts?" *Journal of Marriage and Family* 65 (2003): 539-549.
10. David Popenoe, "Cohabitation, Marriage and Child Well-Being: A Cross-National Perspective," The National Marriage Project, July 7, 2009. For a review of these theories, see Scott M. Stanley, G. K. Rhoades and H. J. Markman, "Sliding Versus Deciding: Inertia and the Premarital Cohabitation Effect," *Family Relations* 55 (2006): 499-509.
11. "Put Him Down as 'Uncommitted'," *The Wall Street Journal*, July 9, 2013.

The 7 Cs

Love is patient; love is kind; love is not envious or boastful or arrogant or rude.... It bears all things, believes all things, hopes all things, endures all things.

1 CORINTHIANS 13:4-5,7

Exercise

Rate the best reason to get married:

1. Looks
2. Loyalty
3. Sense of Humor
4. Wealth
5. Fun
6. Spiritual depth
7. Nice Car
8. Character
9. Hormones
10. Sex appeal

What did you pick? We all have a mental or even a literal list of what we are looking for in a spouse. Let me suggest seven qualities that should be high on your list as you look for compatibility and value in a spouse. I call these the 7 Cs.

1. Character

Character is the moral thermometer of a person's integrity. "Character" is the word used to define a person's good ethics, decency, honor, virtue. A person with character doesn't only *know* what is the right thing to do; he or she actually *does* the right thing.

Anyone worth marrying should have strong character. The spouse-to-be should score high marks in honesty. Integrity always goes a long way, even if he is always watching football or she talks a bit too much.

You can't ever sell short a person who has integrity. If you find that your date lies and can't keep promises, your hand can't move fast enough to hit the eject button.

If he's always looking at other women while he's with you, if she's always flirting with other men while on a date with you—that is a character issue. If he hits you, that's a character issue. If he doesn't pay you back, that's a character issue. Anytime she says one thing and does another, that's a character issue. These characteristics should be so obviously troubling, but it is amazing how a person can overlook the lies, the broken promises, when he or she is infatuated.

Scan for honesty anyone you date as if you're using radar. Or to use a different metaphor, you can't sonar ping someone enough in the early stages of dating to see if he or she is a man or woman of integrity. If someone has an anger issue it doesn't mean an automatic red card and ejection from the game. But if someone has no desire to change or get help, that is a character issue.

One element of integrity is whether the person seems to have a healthy self-awareness of his or her faults, foibles and failures. Is the person always trying to put himself in the best light (which is normal for the first few dates)? Does the person share some of his or her failures? We all have shortcomings. So when will he (or she) reveal them? And in sharing faults, is there a cover-up on the extent or lack of a full disclosure? Way before you get to the engagement, there should be a full disclosure of any issue or challenge—alcoholism, abuse, molestations, bankruptcy, previous marriage, affairs, and the like.

Hear me clearly: I am not saying that if you are an alcoholic, you have a character issue. I am saying that if you hide that area from someone you are dating, with whom you have a clear intent to commit, that is a character issue. No one is perfect. But on the character issue, your analytical nature had better be up and fully functional.

2. Chemistry

Chemistry is the almost unexplainable symbiotic relationship of two people who, when they are together, experience a chemical reaction—a pizzaz, a sizzle, a strong physical attraction for each other. It's the wow factor.

This one is the most subjective element when it comes to being with a romantic other.

Sometimes a relationship is so logical, rational and unemotional that one wonders if this is romance or just a collegial relationship. There's got to be some spark, some magnetism that turns you on about the other person.

Okay, so physical attraction shouldn't necessarily be the highest priority and the only reason to get married. But, even if it is number 2 or number 3, it is still really high! You can't be a Mr. Spock and stay only logical with romance. And even Spock in the movies has the hots for Lieutenant Uhura. Now, physical attraction doesn't always happen on the first date. I thought my wife was gorgeous on our first date. For my wife, I think her positive view of me didn't happen until the second month of dating! We were getting to know each other, but I think it was when she realized that I had fulfilled one of her core values that she allowed herself to let her feelings open toward me.

There comes a point when you watch two people that you can see they move together as a couple. Like a figure skating couple— they glide and skate together. I do not have the gift of matchmaking, so don't come to me to find someone for you. But I think I do have a gift of being with a couple over coffee or a Coke and predicting whether or not they will have a fulfilling and healthy marriage. One of the things I look for is if they move together as a couple. Do they listen to and affirm each other, or are they just two independent people who happen to be dating and like each other? Some couples seem so distant; for others the chemistry is apparent. There needs to be some pizzazz and pride in the other person. There needs to be a strong attraction.

3. Competency

Competency in a person is apparent when he or she shows some ability to master something well. Competent people are seen as efficient, adept, skilled in working with people and in finishing projects.

The person you marry must show a level of competency in life skills. Can he keep a job? Does she show herself to be responsible? Does she know how to handle money? Does he know how to relate to a boss and coworkers in an effective communication style?

Why marry someone who keeps failing in a job? Why hitch up with someone who has a low level of social skills? If becoming a parent is important to you, does this possible mate show a reasonable amount of raw ability to like kids, spend time with kids and act as a good parent?

Does he or she have the organizational skill to run a household? Can you tell that he or she is able to keep out of significant debt? Whatever is important to you, does your future spouse have the competency to do it?

Marriage is the management of one of the most important relationships in the world. It requires a certain kind of competency of interpersonal skills that involves communication, forgiveness, grace, encouragement and introspection. Does your significant other demonstrate that competency?

4. Culture

Culture is the milieu that has developed how we think and operate. It is the background and backdrop of our ethnicity and nationality. Culture is the environment in which we were raised. It is the atmosphere or attitude of what we think is normal or proper.

For a successful marriage to work, one needs to be aware of a potential spouse's cultural background. I don't mean there should not be any cultural differences, but if the gap is too wide it might lead to severe misunderstandings.

Here are several cultural areas one should be aware of to see if there is symmetry between two people—or if the canyon of differences is so great that it could be a problem in marriage:

- Education
- Ethnicity
- Etiquette
- Financial upbringing
- Financial expectations—spending versus saving
- Sophistication in the arts
- Faith

I'm not saying these are divides that can never be bridged, but you need to be aware of a person's culture and assess whether it can work with your own. Let's take education as an example. If one person is a Harvard grad and wants to marry a person who only has a high school education—I would say that is something about which to be careful. It's not impossible to bridge the gap, but it is quite a grand canyon of difference in education, and with that come in-laws and expectations of what success means.

If one person comes from a materially affluent family and the other person comes from a materially disadvantaged background, it might be too great a cultural jump. If a New England Caucasian marries an African American from the South or an East Indian, would it be impossible for such a combination to result in a successful marriage? No. Is it unlikely? I'm not even saying that. Challenging? Yes! Are there great cultural differences? Duh! Just be aware of what each other's culture means and how it will play out in a marriage.

Again, I am not saying there have not been successful marriages of people who are quite different. And I am not saying that interracial marriages are wrong or to be frowned on. Hey, I live in a state that has one of the highest rates of interracial marriages. What I am saying is that you should be aware of how cultural differences raise the bar in smoothing out relationship difficulties. Identify that challenge and be ready to bridge the gap.

There's a great scene in the movie *The Joy Luck Club* where one of the Chinese-American daughters brings home her Caucasian boyfriend, who makes one cultural mistake after another. The narrator in the film describes the series of violations of etiquette: He finishes his entire glass during a toast and pours himself another glass when no one else has had a second glass; he is offered a dish of food that all the guests were to share and takes a huge plateful before anyone else has taken even one helping; he brags about how he is a fast learner and then drops shrimp on his tie while using chopsticks. And then comes the greatest faux pas.

To quote from the movie's dialogue, his girlfriend, as narrator, says, "As is the Chinese cook's custom, my mother always insults her own cooking, but only with the dishes she serves with special pride." The mother says, "This dish not salty enough. No flavor. It's too bad to eat, but please [have some]." Her daughter says, "That was our cue to eat some and proclaim it the best she'd ever made."

The Caucasian boyfriend doesn't know what's going on. Thinking that he is being polite, he says it just needs some soy sauce, thereby confirming the food doesn't have enough flavor. He then pours soy sauce onto the mother's entire dish without even tasting it, and before allowing anyone else to have a serving.

On the drive home, he asks his girlfriend if she brought up to her mother that they want to get married. She says no. He asks why. She replies that her mother "would rather have rectal cancer" than have her marry him.

When two cultures come together who have not had a chance to understand their cultural difference, I am not talking about just ethnic differences, but about educational; financial working class vs. management; Ralph Lauren vs. Old Navy; and so on. If you aren't aware of any cultural differences, you are either blind or just stubborn. If you are unaware of the challenges that come with cultural differences, then you are naive. And if you deny that there are differences between two people even of the same ethnicity, then you are in for a shock.

All of this cautionary advice doesn't mean you should pull the plug on a dating experience if you see *any* differences.

My friends Eric and Jody had what Eric called a "horrible" first date. They went to hear a flute and piano concert. Only 30 people were there. Eric, without awareness that he was doing it, hummed throughout the concert and not even on pitch! Jody looked at him like, *What is wrong with this guy? What kind of bumpkin is this?*

Jody played piano. She was educated in music culture. She went to concerts to hear the music and *just* the music. Eric was a nice local boy from the small town of Wahiawa, Hawaii. Jody was from the East Coast, where her parents were very formal, and they were into cultural and intellectual pursuits. Eric was into passion and emotions—hence the humming. Jody almost decided not to go out with Eric again and to call it off after one date, but she didn't. She gave him another chance. Today, they have one of the best marriages I know. But wait till you read later in this book how they had one of the craziest, most stressful dates I have ever heard of, and it was only about four weeks after this "clash of cultures" date.

5. Commitment

A commitment is a promise, a pledge, an oath; it is a contract one keeps.

Society says that your ability to follow through on a vow determines if you are reliable or not. Making a commitment implies that you have the endurance to weather inconvenience and suffering to make good on what you've said you would do. Marriage is such a commitment. It is about making a vow before God and friends that you intend to keep forever.

Does the person you are thinking of marrying display enough of a track record that he or she could be loyal for a lifetime? If he has been married three times, and all have been short marriages due to divorce, be careful; commitment may not be this guy's strength! If you find out that he has had a number of affairs, don't be a dummy and think, *He will be different with me.* The overarching message of this book is about pulling us all out of infatuation and making sure we have our wits about us.

Commitment is the glue that keeps a relationship stable through thick and thin. Marriage must be based on a covenant for life, not on what you are feeling in the moment. If marriage is based on *feelings,* then it will be a roller-coaster relationship. If your spouse wakes up one day and he doesn't *feel* very warm toward you, does that mean his love for you goes down? And in any given day, if you *feel* good about him, does that mean your love for him goes up? If you wake up one day with a bad hair day, does that mean his affection for you goes down? That's all a bunch of nonsense! True love is not manipulated by changing feelings.

So, why is it so difficult to get that straight? Because so much of what the media tells us is love bases it on feeling. There is the "I love you because" idea, which says, I love you because you are young or healthy or wealthy. There is the "I love you if" idea, which says, I will love you only *if* you do certain things for me. These two describe a *conditional* kind of love. But the love that counts is the "I love you in spite of" idea, which says, I will love you in spite of your weaknesses, failings, age or whatever. This is the love that is unconditional and that is required of us if we want to get married. This kind of love will require all of the character and integrity and faith we have to make that happen.

This kind of commitment means being fully aware of any challenges in the relationship, like the ones I've mentioned with character and culture. And it means making a deliberate commitment based on that clear view of the relationship and the person to whom you are committing.

Commitment equals loyalty. Has your mate-to-be a track record of loyalty? The cousins of loyalty are patience, endurance and stick-to-itiveness. Anyone who easily quits a job or task or who plays the victim or the blame game is a poor candidate for loyalty. The Bible says that if you are faithful in the little things, then you will be faithful in the big things (see Luke 19:17). Watch how your friend is faithful and keeps promises in the small things, especially when no one is looking. That is a great window to view how he or she would commit to marriage.

6. Communication

Communication is not a one-way street. It comprises both sending and receiving messages—what you say and how the other person hears what you say, and vice versa. It is the way we reveal what we are thinking and also how we determine what the other person is thinking. It's the style of how we affirm, forgive, encourage or divulge information. Communication takes place in conversation, letter writing, emails, phone calls and nonverbal body language. All of these elements of communication are a vital part of any relationship.

As you look at the person you are dating (or thinking of dating), what is the pattern of behavior you observe when it comes to communication style? For example, take conflict resolution. In the face of an argument or disagreement, does the person go into a rage, get defensive, pout, go silent, get passive-aggressive, become violent or throw things? If these reactions are well-established patterns, they will be very hard to change inside of a marriage. These communication themes go on for a long time.

When there is disagreement, does this person say that maybe it is his fault? Does she forgive or does she hold grudges? Does she listen or is she an interrupter? Does he keep short accounts before things can go longer and get too deep to address? Does she seem to know how to forgive?

I remember sociologist Tony Campolo saying to me that when he did counseling, if one person blamed the other person for all the wrong done, Tony didn't feel much hope for the couple. But if ever one person said, "Maybe I am the one who did something wrong. I need to change, but I don't know how . . ." And the other replied, "Maybe I screwed up on this one," then he felt the couple had a lot of hope of making it, because there was humility in the communication style.

Humility is a great test of good communication as well as character. Communication is something you will always need to work on in a marriage, so the dating period is a good time to lay a foundation of asking for what you want in a nonthreatening way and truly listening to and understanding what the other person is saying before you formulate your response. Good listeners almost always have good marriages because they know that communication is as much about the other person's view as it is about one's own.

7. Core Values

Everyone has core values they hold dear. Core values are basic and fundamental to who a person is. They are the foundation for what brings a person joy and passion. They determine what a person thinks is right and wrong in life.

Do you and the person you are dating share some basic core values? If supporting the Democratic party is important to you, is the person you are dating of the same view? If it is important to you to have a heart for the poor, does she have one too? If you think it's important to save the environment, does he agree? If your faith is of utmost importance, does he put the same value on faith? If you want to live simply, does he want the same thing? If you want the best of everything, does she want it too? And can you afford it?

I'm a Christian pastor. I tell people that if you are a follower of Jesus, if He is the most important person in your life, if He is the one you have passion for and trust, and you center your life on Him, then you had better marry a Christian. It's just the practical thing to do; because if you don't, it is only a matter of time before you move apart. Think about it this way: If two jets are flying parallel to each other, but one changes course just one degree, it is only a matter of time before that one degree will result in thousands of miles between the two jets. So it is with marriage. If you decide to be off by one degree in a core value, it will only be a matter of time until you become far apart from each other. To be sure, no two people are exactly on course all the time; but if you are 30 degrees off on a core value, buyer beware.

I have found that for a Christian who marries either a non-Christian or a Christian of a far less devout degree, most of the time the faith of the couple gravitates toward the lowest common denominator. If one-half of the couple doesn't want to go to church, both will eventually stop going to church, stop reading the Bible, and stop praying as much. Or they find that it can be a subject of division. If there are kids in the family, it raises issues such as, will they go to church, and what are the family's goals in this area?

Let's again take the core value of religion and apply it to both people in a dating relationship or in marriage.

If both are followers of Jesus and have read the Bible, they will have a similar approach to forgiveness. They have an understanding and a standard operating procedure of whom to forgive and why it is so important.

For the Christian, he/she has learned that forgiveness means to give up the right to retaliate in any way—in thought or in deed. If there is going to be any "vengeance," it is left to God to make that happen, because none of us knows in our humanness what proper retaliation would be. And if there is conflict, then one should seek help from God.

However, a secular person may feel that if someone hurts you, then you hurt the person back. He says, "Revenge is my right; I can give the person who hurt me the silent treatment or throw out hurtful words in a raised voice to penalize the person." These different approaches to the same problem depend on a person's core value.

If both people are Christ-followers, they will have a similar passion to pray together and help the poor, to share their faith with others and attempt to forgive others as we have been forgiven, as the Lord's Prayer says (see Matthew 6:12). At the very least, they will have a common set of ethics they will attempt to follow and use as a guide when they fail. They will have a similar philosophy of generosity and giving to the church and to Christian causes.

Pick whatever topic you would write down for core values. But know that if you and your intended differ in a core value—even by a few degrees—in the long run there is significant potential for greater differences in passion that might lead to both doing their own thing, or a lessening of passion in order to meet the one with the lower passion.

I have used faith as an example of a core value. Insert whatever other core value speaks to your life—travel, ecology, tennis, living in the South, social justice, environment, to name just a few. Make it your priority to define your core values so that you can easily see if another person is close enough to them or is traveling the few degrees apart that will eventually create too much distance to allow you to come together again.

Study Questions

1. Which of the 7 Cs of relationship compatibility make the most sense to you?

   _____

   _____

   _____

   _____

2. Which of the 7 Cs surprised you to see it on the list? Why?

   _____

   _____

   _____

   _____

3. What traits would you add to the compatibility list?

   _____

   _____

   _____

   _____

4. What new understanding did you receive from the definition of "communication" and its importance?

   _____

   _____

   _____

   _____

5. What new awareness now informs you about what might have gone wrong in a past relationship? How have you prioritized your core values as a result of that awareness?

   _____

   _____

   _____

   _____

My Premarital Advice

I see God in the instruments and the mechanisms that work reliably.

R. BUCKMINSTER FULLER, "GOD IS A VERB"

I have performed hundreds of marriages, but not without thoroughly counseling a couple pre-marriage. I felt it was my duty to run them through the gauntlet. I mentioned in chapter 2 that I required any couple that wanted me to perform their marriage to meet with me three times for an hour each appointment. It was mandatory that they fill out an inventory (see Appendix B); take the Myers-Briggs Type Indicator (a personality test also called Keirsey-Bates); and the 225-question Edwards Personal Preference Schedule that asks the test taker, among other things, what are the needs in his or her life in terms of dominance, order, need to feel guilty, achievement, affiliation with friends, endurance, decision making, desire for sex and so on.

I felt it was my duty to run them through the gauntlet. Remember, it was my assumption and theory that most couples (not all) were highly infatuated and naïve as to what marriage is all about. I couldn't blame them since they had either never been married or already had experienced a failed marriage. They were also typically on cloud nine and on their best behavior with one another.

The inventory was to see if they truly had a sense of who they were as individuals, and what they truly knew about their partner. I asked them about their parents' marriage because, rightly or wrongly, their parents would provide the strongest model of what a marriage should or shouldn't be like. And sometimes, in spite of their best efforts to do things differently, they were bound to repeat some of what they saw their parents do. It's why people often say,

"I can't believe I'm doing just what my parents used to do, and I said I'd never do that."

The inventory zeroed in on critical areas that would play a major part in the couples' marriage. It asked about their parents: What do you like about your parents' relationship, and dislike about it? It asked the couple about whether they had experienced previous counseling, drug treatment or an arrest. What were the issues? How did they perceive the strengths and weaknesses of their spouse-to-be? Was there a prenuptial agreement? Why did they have such an agreement? Was anyone in debt? How much debt? Would there be a budget? And so on.

These tests were for the couple's compatibility. But even more so, I was trying to inform them of what their own personalities were like. I was trying to make them aware of differences and how they might consider strategies to overcome them. Sometimes, if there had been abuse or molestation in the past, the counseling was to warn the couple how sex and life in general might need extra sensitivity and gentleness due to the history of the fiancé(e).

My first session with a couple was usually quite challenging. I wanted to shake them up to make sure they knew what they were getting into and move them away from infatuation (i.e., "I am marrying the perfect man in the world who understands all of my needs") to the reality that he or she would be marrying an imperfect sinner, just like them. Some marriages were never meant to be. And I knew that if a bad marriage could be avoided, it would feel like a bullet had been dodged and blessings had come down instead.

Just the fact that premarital counseling was required may very well have increased the chances for a couple's successful marriage. A study showed that premarital counseling gives you greater odds for a stronger, more successful marriage. Research evaluated 23 different studies on the effectiveness of premarital counseling, and the findings showed that couples with premarital counseling and education reported a 30 percent stronger marriage than other couples. The researchers said their findings suggested that if you want to have a strong, lifelong marriage, premarital counseling is a good investment.[1]

I like what Seth Myers wrote in a *Psychology Today* article:

Why so many couples avoid premarital counseling—or counseling early in the marriage for that matter—has to do with
fear.... Though it can be scary to vent your anger, frustration
and resentments, it is the release of these feelings in a struc-
tured context that actually allows two people to move past
them and later start liking each other again.[2]

I strongly, strongly recommend that all couples that have dated
for a while, or are engaged, go to premarital counseling. It is bene-
ficial to have an objective third party point out any blind spots you
might not see.

After going over a couple's family history and psychological
test scores (this was all free—the amazing benefit of being part of a
church!), I normally went over several points. What follows are the
highlights of what I taught in premarital counseling sessions and
during our public teachings and special retreats.

When Circumstances Abruptly Change

Don't marry a person unless (perish the thought!) on the day after your marriage, after a traffic accident causes your husband to
become quadriplegic, you would still choose to stay married to the
person. I included this example to make sure the counselee knew
she was marrying someone *based on a love for him and not just a "like."*
I wanted to make sure the couple had an abiding love, and that each
would stand by the other and be loyal and serve one another.

Part of this challenge came from a true story about a young
missionary couple in a church I attended. The couple suffered great
hardship when a car hit the man soon after the wedding. He ended
up in a wheelchair for life. I was amazed at how the wife remained
loyal to him even though things had changed so quickly and drastically from what their initial hopes and dreams were. That kind of
commitment is the stuff of which marriage should be made.

Money Can't Buy You Love or Commitment

Have you ever wished, with some degree of longing, that you were as
rich as, and had as much help as, the royals in England? I remember

when Prince Charles and Lady Diana got married in 1981 (the same year my wife of 30-plus years and I got married). The Archbishop of Canterbury said, "This is the stuff of which fairy tales are made." Ah yes, the dashing prince sweeps a beautiful lady off her feet, and they live in a castle with riches and land forever and ever. But it was just a fairy tale—their longevity as a couple was short-lived.

It turned out that there was infidelity—even on their wedding day—as the prince still loved another woman who eventually became his second wife (Lady Camilla). Behind the glitter and glamour and riches, there was heartache, depression, sadness, affairs and then, finally, the death of Princess Diana as she and her boyfriend died in a car crash in France.

Speaking of the need for commitment, wrap your head around this: When you look at the British royals, you have to realize they have almost anything they want and could use those resources to help take the stress off of a marriage. They have tons of money. They have servants who clean their dishes and homes and take their pets out to relieve themselves and get shampooed. They don't work for any boss. They can go on exotic vacations. They don't have to worry about food on the table or what to wear, and their valets dress them, and they have chauffeurs and security men. Whenever they want to go on a date, they can just do it and someone will watch the kids. Free baby-sitting whenever they want. They have all that. All that!

And yet, time and time again royals have affairs and mess up their lives and have unhappy marriages. All the money and the fame and timesaving benefits in the world won't buy you happiness. It also takes commitment, loyalty and a strong desire to communicate.

So it's just myth to think that if only you had a lot of money or help or a less stressful job, then you would have a happy marriage. Nothing beats old-fashioned commitment, communication and a heart to serve one another.

Choosing the 60/40 Rule

Speaking of serving one another, you will hear people say that marriage is always 50/50—if the husband does his part and the wife does hers, all will be happy. That is a lie.

A successful marriage cultivates a 60/40 attitude. Go into the marriage expecting to pour in 60 percent to your spouse's 40 percent. If your spouse should put in 50 percent, then hey, you got more than you bargained for, and that is icing on the cake. If your spouse only puts in 40 percent (at least according to you), you knew that when you got married. And you knew that you were committed to be the primary server.

But imagine if both of you try to put in 60 percent, and both of you are trying to out-serve each other and out-forgive each other! Then you will enjoy a happy, fulfilled, servant-like marriage.

Don't enter marriage to be fulfilled, because you will always want to be served rather than serve. You will always seek to be made complete. Instead, get married to fulfill the other person. If you say, "I am marrying him because he makes me feel complete," you will always want to be on the receiving end and will look for ways for him to fill in that "missing puzzle piece" to make you happy. This is a recipe for disaster!

The way to think about marriage is to work on a lifestyle of giving before receiving. It will cultivate goodwill in all relationships, whether dating or marriage. Relationships should not be "transactional"—if I do this for you, then you have to do this for me. That's more like a business deal; I scratch your back, so you had better scratch mine.

If both spouses work on trying to figure out how the other person will find more joy, more purpose, more success, then the ingredients for a great marriage are there. Both are trying to outdo the other in doing good. The Bible says, "Do not become weary in doing good" (Galatians 6:9, NIV). This is a great passage for marriage, among other things. Memorize it and use it to remember the 60/40 rule.

One of my favorite passages to read at a wedding speaks of Christ's servanthood. It is a great model for marriage:

> If then there is any encouragement in Christ, any consolation from love, any sharing in the Spirit, any compassion and sympathy, make my joy complete: be of the same mind, having the same love, being in full accord and of

one mind. Do nothing from selfish ambition or conceit, but in humility regard others as better than yourselves. Let each of you look not to your own interests, but to the interests of others. Let the same mind be in you that was in Christ Jesus, who, though he was in the form of God, did not regard equality with God as something to be exploited, but emptied himself, taking the form of a slave, being born in human likeness. And being found in human form, he humbled himself and became obedient to the point of death—even death on a cross (Philippians 2:1-8).

Sometimes It's Better to Be Single

I know there are a lot of single people out there wishing they were married. Many singles will never get married. But, believe me, to be married and unhappy is a lot more painful. Lonely, as a single? Try loneliness inside a marriage. That is excruciating.

Exercise

Which state of being is worse?

1. Happily married
2. Happily single
3. Unhappily single
4. Unhappily married

I truly believe that *D* is the answer.

The key point is that if you marry the wrong person, then life can be very, very hard. So choose well. I say, *Unhappily single is better than unhappily married.* The constant reminder in an unhappy marriage is that you are not lovable or desirable. This can drive your self-esteem way down. It's like a pile driver that pounds concrete piles into the ground for a multistory building. It's constant, hard-hitting and noisy. In an unhappy marriage, your self-esteem gets pushed down farther and farther. It puts you so low that it creates a foundation of low self-esteem.

In a surprising article by Jeanie Lerche Davis titled "Women:
Single and Loving it," she analyzes the question "Are women better
off alone?" She discovers that marriage is not the perfect formula
for happiness. She quotes the social psychologist at the University
of California Santa Barbara, Dr. Bella DePaulo. Lerche writes:

> Marriage isn't a magic bullet for a wonderful life, says De-
> Paulo. "But it has that appeal that you will meet this person
> and everything falls into place. Yet if you look to one per-
> son to be everything, it's not fair to that person, not fair to
> you, and it's not healthy. And if the marriage doesn't last,
> it's devastating."
>
> One study tracking 1,000 couples for 15 years found
> that marriage brought only a "tiny blip" of happiness
> during the brief time closest to the wedding ceremony. "But
> on average, afterwards, people go back to the way they were
> before. The researcher's perspective is that we each have a
> baseline of happiness, and marriage on average isn't going
> to change that—except for that little blip," DePaulo says.
>
> In fact, most married vs. single "happiness studies" are
> seriously flawed, she adds. "They lump all single people
> together—divorced, widowed, always-single—without fac-
> toring in the transition period, the really unnerving period
> in your life after divorce or becoming widowed," she tells
> WebMD. "Over time, you go back to the person you were
> before. But studies don't take that transition period into
> account."[3]

If you are single, you may think that getting married will make
you so much happier. Not necessarily. Studies seem to say that you
go back to the person you were when single. It's not, "I am miserable
now, but I will get married to be a happily married person." If you
are miserable now and always see the cup as half empty, you may
be miserable and see the cup as half empty in marriage too. If you
have a pessimistic personality, you will probably bring that with you
into marriage. Marriage is not a magic bullet. Therefore, it is really
good to know yourself.

Always Be the Real You

Know yourself. Be yourself. I think many singles focus on finding the right person. I think the most successful matches result in being yourself and letting the other person find and be attracted to the real you, as opposed to putting on a show and having someone be attracted to a false you that you have to keep pretending to be. Of course, dating is courtship, but don't try to be something you're not, even when dating.

If you are unhappy now, will marriage really transform you, or just make you avoid issues you need to deal with as a single? The temptation is to act like the kind of person your partner would like. But if you do that, he falls in love with a mirage. Be the person you like. And work on those things you need to deal with before marriage.

Get Rid of the Lengthy, Unreasonable Wish List for Your Ideal Mate

It's fun to make the wish list, and it's important to have criteria and not lower your standards. But make sure you are not being too much of a perfectionist when it comes to searching for a mate. There was only one Jesus, and He's not available. Only one Virgin Mary, and she's not here.

But here's the deal: Do you know why marriage is the hardest relationship in the world—harder than a college roommate or an apartment or house roommate? In marriage, we discover how sinful we really are. We live with someone on a *constant* basis who sees how really selfish and self-centered we can be. It is only a matter of time until the masks come off.

We cannot hide our sinfulness from a mate. So some of the questions we should have on a list for selecting a mate are: How does he or she handle disappointment? How does she or he handle conflict resolution or receiving or giving forgiveness? Where is that person on the spectrum of patience and understanding when your friend that you hope becomes your spouse sees you as you really are—sinful at the core. Go ahead and make a list, but this is the challenging question: Are *you* becoming the person you want to marry?

Work on Being the Person You Want to Marry

Many singles make a list of what they want in a spouse.

I want someone who:

- loves God
- prays a lot
- forgives
- loves unconditionally
- does a lot of volunteer work

And who is:

- physically fit
- flexible and easygoing
- a good conversationalist

But the question is, are *you* that person? I used to laugh (inside) when someone would tell me in a counseling session that they wanted someone who prays a lot and knows the Bible and goes all out for God 24/7.

And then I would gently ask, "Are you the kind of person you want to marry? Do you pray a lot?" The person would say no. "Do you really know the Bible?" The person would say no. "Are you going all-out for God and trying to live a godly life 24/7?" And again, the person would look down and say, "Uh, no." "You want someone who has a great body and who is easy to be with, but are you physically fit? Are you easygoing?" And on and on.

The right question is, Would a person want to marry *you* with the qualities *you* have? If the answer is no, then this is a good time to improve yourself and be the kind of person you would want to marry. Like attracts like. Be the kind of person you want to date, and start focusing on it now. It might take time to develop some of the qualities you desire in others.

In the end, when choosing a spouse, it is not necessarily about finding the right healthy person but *becoming* the right healthy person. Whether or not you get married, at least you will have become the person God wanted you to be and are living a life with all of the gifts and skills and talents He planned for you to display.

If you know you are the person with the qualities you are looking for in a mate, how do you find that person you want to marry?

Where Do I Go? What Do I Do?

If like attracts like, what are the watering holes where the kind of person you like would go? If you want someone who loves environmental causes or social justice projects, then get involved in such things. Want a Christian mate? Go to Christian events or gathering places where Christians would be—church, Bible studies, small groups, work projects, missions projects. It's not fair to complain to God that you can't meet anyone you like if you are not moving around to meet people. A car in neutral is not going forward. And if it's on a hill, it might even go backward! Go to safe places where singles may gather.

What about Internet dating? There is nothing wrong with that, and many of the services are geared toward certain kinds of people. Some of the sites have you write essays that might reveal more about you (and you can read about the other person) before you arrange a possible meeting time. (More on that later.)

Playing the Odds

When you start looking at statistics, you can make some crazy assumptions. The Barna Group reported in a national survey of over 5,000 adults (over 3,700 were married) that the most prolific experience of marriage ending in divorce takes place among these groups:

- Downscale (not a college graduate, making less than $20,000) adults—39%
- Baby Boomers—38%
- Those aligned with non-Christian faith—38%
- People who consider themselves liberal on social/political matters—37%
- African Americans—36%
- Protestant—34%
- White—32%
- Hispanic—31%

- Catholics—28%
- Evangelical—26%
- Upscale Adults—22%
- Asians—20%[4]

So, judging from the last three categories, if you could find an upscale-evangelical-Asian, you are into beating the odds! (Okay, full disclaimer: My daughter and sons are single, upscale, evangelical Asians, but no, you can't date them.)

So where does God come into the picture?

Does God Have a Perfect Mate in Mind for You?

This is a most controversial question. It really has to do with your theology of providence. Do you believe everything in your life has been directed or allowed by God? And even if you have chosen the wrong person, did God allow that for some other reason? This is a very important issue but not one you can ever prove. *Only in hindsight will you know if you married the right person.*

I believe that God does have someone specific in mind for us to marry. But even if you believe that, it doesn't mean your marriage will be easy. Maybe God gave you someone who had a bad childhood and is insecure, and He chose you to help that person. The "right" marriage doesn't guarantee that you will have a happy life. Maybe God allows your marriage to be less than ideal for a divine purpose. Joseph, for example, was sold into slavery. He suffered for 13 years. He was falsely accused of sexual harassment. But it was all part of a plan that would save his family from a famine that would have killed all of them. (You can read the entire amazing story in the book of Genesis, chapters 37–47.)

Whether a difficult or fulfilling marriage, the main point is to truly seek God's will in finding a mate. And if in your heart you believe that you have found the right person, then in faith stay committed to that person, even through hell and high water. In that sense, whoever you have married *is* God's choice. So stay faithful to the person you marry, even if it's tough. You can't unscramble eggs. In the Old Testament (see the book of Hosea), God told His prophet Hosea to marry Gomer, who was unfaithful; Hosea stayed with her. By doing so, Hosea lived out a life of covenant and promise. God calls us to live a life of covenant and promise too.

Does God have His best choice of a spouse for us? I believe He does. But if you're in a difficult marriage, hang in there. It doesn't mean you have chosen the wrong person just because the marriage is hard. It still may be God's choice for you. Are there reasons to get out of a marriage? Not many, but yes, these reasons exist (adultery, desertion, violence, severe addictions that deplete finances, and child abuse, to name a few). The bottom line is that you should go into marriage without any plans to leave.

In the hundreds of marriages I have performed, the couples who signed a prenuptial agreement in case it didn't work out *all* ended up divorced. *If you build a back door, you will use it every time.* You can't be kind of committed any more than you can be kind of pregnant. A prenuptial to protect yourself because you are unsure about the person you are marrying is not a wise thing to do. If you are unsure, then don't marry.

I would say, however, that a prenuptial is okay to protect the inheritance of children from a first marriage, or when one spouse has passed and it would be honorable to preserve the legacy of the departed as planned during the first marriage.

You must go into marriage believing by faith that you have chosen the right one; that you are marrying God's choice for you. If the community has agreed with you on the choice, and you have really given them the permission to tell you their true feelings, and you have really sought God's will and prayed and talked to the spiritually mature in your community, then there is a very good chance you are marrying God's choice.

But one of the greatest ways to find the right spouse is up to you.

Know Thyself

The greatest advantage you can have in picking the right spouse is in knowing yourself. If you truly know yourself and how you tick, then you have a better chance to choose the right mate for life. Your prayers will be clearer. Your friends will be able to confirm the match better as you reveal who you are in strengths and weaknesses.

It's hard to fully know yourself. But let me tell you why it is key. Often, we unconsciously choose a spouse to make up for those deficient areas of our childhood or adolescence. Let's start with parents. Though it may sound like the Greek tragic figure Oedipus, who unknowingly married his mother, we often are unknowingly marrying someone exactly like our mother or father in an attempt to make up for what we wanted from him or her. That is why, in my premarital counseling, I always ask questions about the couples' parents. Rightly or wrongly, our parents are our best models of how a marriage should be or should not be. Sometimes we want to emulate our parents' relationship and copy it; or perhaps we don't want anything to do with it.

The role model you witnessed in your parents' marriage can be a two-edged sword. Sometimes when you see that your parents were not good communicators, you strive to talk to your spouse in a more healthy way. That is good. But if you didn't have a model of how that is done, you don't always know how to communicate in a good way. Or, if your father yelled a lot, you might be hypersensitive to yelling in your marriage. So you need to know where that sensitivity is coming from in order to make a change.

Sometimes it is a bit more complicated. We seek a spouse to fill in for what we did not get from our parents. If we didn't get enough affirmation from our mother and father, we may want our husband/wife to be that constant affirmer. We think this is a normal thing to ask for. When we strive for that verbal affirmation or focus on it too much, we might be hypersensitive when we don't get it. Whatever it is that happened to you with your parents in childhood, you bring that baggage into your marriage.

I've encountered some examples of such baggage in my years of premarital counseling, and they're emblematic of the hurdles many couples can face:

- Susan's father molested her when she was young. Having sex with her spouse was not easy because of the bad memories attached to sex from her childhood.
- Bob's father left him and his mom at an early age and then his mom died when he was 16. Abandonment

issues were big for Bob, and whenever his girlfriend unexpectedly had to change plans with him, he felt unwar-
ranted feelings of betrayal and desertion.

- Kathy's father never praised her accomplishments.
When she got an A- in a class, he asked her why not an
A? So she found throughout life that she was always trying to achieve more and more and do more and more.
- Terry tried to commit suicide and failed. In the first family meeting with one of our pastors, Terry's father said,
"And he couldn't even do that right." With the lack of
a father's blessing, understanding, empathy or affirmation, Terry would always question whether someone really loved him, and he felt hesitant to share his weaknesses.

We all have had experiences that are emotional hurdles to clear,
even if they might not have been as intense as these examples. This
means that you really do need to know yourself—to acknowledge
your experiences and consider how they continue to affect you
today—before you get married or else you will be in for a much
more difficult marriage. When you do not know yourself, you will
continually look for someone who will fill in all of the areas where
you feel incomplete.

Guess what? *No one will ever fill the void you have for the love you
want or need. No one. Only God can do that.* The fact is that we all have
a terminal illness called sin. We are so imperfect and selfish at our
core that it's unrealistic to think that putting two imperfect, selfish, sinful people together will guarantee a perfect marriage. If you
can come to the conclusion *before* you get married that the person
you walk down the aisle with is not perfect, that he is not Jesus,
not a saint, and that only God can fulfill your deepest needs, then
you are headed into the healthiest courtship and marriage of all.

A wedding day can be one of the most unrealistic days of a
person's life. Men who typically manifest sketchy grooming hab-
its—unkempt or greasy hair, and who wear T-shirts and shorts or
jeans—are now spiffed up and wearing a tuxedo or a handsome
suit. Women have make-up applied that they would never wear
in daily life. Relatives are smiling and laughing. People are giving

verbal testimonies of affirmation and appreciation like never be-fore—it's the kind of language usually reserved for eulogies. You are the center of attention as cameras flash and pop all over as if you were a movie star. You eat at a fine restaurant or hotel or at a scenic picnic area. You dine at prices you rarely would sign up for. This is the most unrealistic, self-indulgent, narcissistic view of married life, and yet that is how we start a marriage. Some people think that is what marriage will be like forever.

I want to say that only God is the perfect, forgiving, wise, pro-tective affirmer that we all desire in the deepest part of our hearts. Don't expect that of your spouse. You aren't in that perfect arena either. Whether you are single or married, you need to grow into and arrive at that place where you realize that God is so personal and so loving and so there for you that you could echo the words of King David from Psalm 23:

> The LORD is my shepherd, I shall not want.
> He makes me lie down in green pastures;
> he leads me beside still waters;
> he restores my soul.
> He leads me in right paths
> for his name's sake.
>
> Even though I walk through the darkest valley,
> I fear no evil;
> for you are with me;
> your rod and your staff—
> they comfort me.
>
> You prepare a table before me
> in the presence of my enemies;
> you anoint my head with oil;
> my cup overflows.
> Surely goodness and mercy shall follow me
> all the days of my life,
> and I shall dwell in the house of the LORD
> my whole life long.

King David—a macho ruler, general, shepherd—knew that God was the only one who could make sure he never wanted for anything else. It was God who would give him the peace of green pastures near still, calm waters. He would never need to be afraid, even in the valley of death. It was God who would guide him with a shepherd's rod and staff, who would be with him for his whole life long.

What we tried to do in that Menlo Park church community was to get centered on God first, to know Him personally as Jesus here on earth and then we would have His Holy Spirit in us to center us on the only One who could love us the way we would want to be loved. That's where it has to start. You do not pass Go and collect $200 if God is not part of the deal.

So, go into a courtship with your eyes open. Courtship is a testing time to see if it means marriage or break-up. Those are the only two options. You are a sinner; you are dating a sinner. Some challenges might be too hard to overcome, like cocaine addiction or a deep insecurity. But some strengths are worth gold, and you can move forward toward that kind of person.

As pastor and author Tim Keller once said (using an Old Testament reference from Genesis 29, where Jacob's bride, unknowingly to him, got switched out on his wedding day with her sister), in marriage we go to bed thinking our spouse is the beautiful Rebecca, and we wake up to find her sister, the plain Leah. We have married a sinner, and there is no exception. The more we realize that we are all "Leahs," and only God is perfect, the better chance we have of picking a realistic spouse.

Study Questions

1. Do you agree with the idea that every couple moving toward marriage needs premarital counseling? Why, or why not?

_____

_____

_____

2. If you were to have premarital counseling, what would be your greatest fear?

_____

_____

_____

3. Which of the premarital advice points make the most sense to you?

_____

_____

_____

4. We all look for a mate who will fill in what is missing in us unless we do what? Do you agree that God is the only one who will ever fill that role?

_____

_____

_____

5. Do you believe that God has the perfect mate for you? Why, or why not? Do you have the same qualities that you are looking for in a mate?

_____

_____

_____

Notes
1. "Premarital Counseling Builds Better Union: Counseling Before Marriage Makes Couples Stronger," WebMD, April 4, 2003. http://women.webmd.com/news/20030404/premarital-counseling-builds-better-union (accessed November 2013).
2. Seth Myers, *Psychology Today*, September 21, 2011.
3. Jeanie Lerche Davis, "Women: Single and Loving it," WebMD, quoting Dr. Bella DePaulo from the University of California Santa Barbara. http://www.webmd.com/sex-relationships/features/single-and-loving-it (accessed December 2013).
4. The Barna Group, March 31, 2008.

Antivirus Software

Dictators don't take vacations.
BERNARD-HENRI LEVI, FRENCH PHILOSOPHER

Nobody loves a Death Star.
PEGGY NOONAN, COLUMNIST

Every computer should be protected with antivirus software. And every relationship should have a set of warning signs akin to antivirus software. This chapter speaks of several yellow-flag traits to be aware of when detected in a person you are dating. These traits could point to an unsafe prospect in spouse selection. Granted, no one is perfect; but there are specific threats to a relationship that you can identify before you step into marriage.

Marriage is for a lifetime, so anything you can do to prevent a harmful "virus" from entering your relationship is good. As I said earlier, during the dating period, people are usually on their *best* behavior. If you see signs of these things when dating, be aware that it will probably get more pronounced later. Some of these symptoms or signs may seem small, but like an iceberg, you may only be seeing the tip, and there could be a lot more under the surface.

Even if these traits are not severe enough for you to sever your relationship, at least you have a heads-up on what could be lifelong issues with your spouse. How long do you really want to put up with these things? You don't want to live a life where you are continually compensating. That will drain you. Yes, a big part of marriage requires some compensating and compromising, but there is a limit on that.

Let's look at some of these warning signs that indicate a virus present. Too many of these signs, or too severe a degree of some of them, might be cause to stop the relationship. These signs are not in order of priority, but they are all key areas of concern.

1. Stinginess

You might be surprised that being stingy even made the list. But if you detect during your dating that the person you are with continually shows signs of stinginess (as opposed to generosity), it could indicate how he will treat you in marriage. If she is a penny-pincher while out at a restaurant or in purchasing items or in entertainment, be aware that there is a fine line between frugality and stinginess.

Stinginess is *unnecessarily* not spending on something because you think you don't deserve it or it limits the celebration of life. Or stinginess occurs because you have a fear of the unknown, so you hoard things and money like a packrat.

I know of a marriage in which the husband gives an allowance to his wife and decides how much she can spend. You may find this hard to believe, but there are some husbands who limit the allowance to as low as $5 to $25 at a time (and the couple is not living at the poverty level). The wife never saw this coming during the courtship, or refused to acknowledge it. Stinginess can show a lack of trust for a spouse or a lack of trust in God's ability to take care of us.

Having done a lot of marriage counseling, it is not surprising to hear that couples fight about money. Money management (or the lack of money) is a primary topic of conflict, because the use of money can lead to frustration or fulfillment. Is it not profound that Jesus said that the *love* of money, not money itself, is a root of all kinds of evil (see 1 Timothy 6:10)? Stinginess is a form of "the love of money." This includes wanting to keep it so that others won't be blessed. In addition, the wrong attitude about money can incite a person to steal, embezzle, and be motivated by greed.

Nothing is wrong with frugality and saving money. In general, people should save more. But stinginess caps off fun, joy, generous hospitality, gratitude for gifts, having a heart for the poor, and supporting ministry and charity. Signs of stinginess can be seen in how we tip, buy clothes for ourselves, give gifts or show gratitude for others. It can also be seen in whether one has a heart for the downtrodden, which includes giving money to those in need.

Stinginess is also a sign of a lack of faith in God's ability to bless beyond measure. In reality, you can't out-give God, and He is a debtor to no one. Stinginess says, "I have to cut back because if I don't do this, God won't either, and I will not live the abundant life."

I was talking to my friend Peter, who was helping me buy a light for my kitchen. I told him that I didn't care how much it costs because I would have to look at the light fixture every day. To which he responded, "That makes sense. When I got married to my wife, Rea, I said, 'I don't care how much you cost because I have to look at you every day.'" It's a funny way of saying it, but your date or your future spouse costs more than a lamp, so be generous with your time or gifts, because your significant other might be with you and see you for the rest of your life. The same applies to you; you are more than a light fixture too.

2. Anger

In some cultures, yelling, grabbing, shoving or hitting a spouse or girlfriend is okay. But if that is how your date treats you, watch out! Physical and verbal violence is never acceptable. Even if you were raised by a father or stepparent who treated you that way, know now, as you read this, that it is unacceptable behavior and never helpful or healthy for a marriage.

Throwing things, swearing at other drivers, cursing out waitresses, screaming, smashing walls with fists or objects are all signs of a person who has little self-control.

I know someone who, on a date in a hotel, yelled at other customers in a bar simply because he was asked to please be a bit quieter and move out of the way of the sports game on TV.

I know of another who, on a date, dressed down the waiter for bringing him a bad-tasting (so he thought) bottle of wine. (Why is that the waiter's fault?)

When dating, these behaviors are yellow flags. Imagine when the couple is no longer dating and the angry partner is no longer on his or her best behavior. In marriage, those yellow flags become red flags.

I know of a woman who was pregnant and was thrown down a flight of stairs by her angry husband.

I know of husbands who have pushed their spouses against walls and choked and kicked them during an argument.

I know of a wife who picked up her husband's computer and threw it on the floor in retaliation during an argument.

If you see any signs of anger or violence, your antivirus software should be sending off blinking lights and warning sounds.

If you put up with someone who is frequently angry with you and the whole world, it might mean that you are codependent, because you tolerate it.

3. Codependency

What is codependency? Marriage and family therapist Tina Tessina says it is basically when you make a relationship more important to you than you are to yourself.[1] Codependency is when you are dependent on the *relationship* (not necessarily the person) for fulfillment. Are you wondering how or why you would ever do that? Codependency slips in subtly with severe consequences. Codependent people don't know it, but they are locked in a death dance where they try to save their partner or the relationship over and over again to the neglect of their own health.

This is evident when one partner is an alcoholic or has other kinds of addictions, and the partner, the codependent one, tries to fix it even to the detriment of his or her own health. A friend said to me, "Codependency is when your friend is drowning and you decide to die." There are no healthy boundaries in codependency. When trying to help someone, you continually act to the detriment of yourself or the relationship.

Eugene and Chrissie were married, but Eugene refused to work or go outside of the house. Even though he was home all day, he would not help with cleaning the house or cooking. Chrissie had to do it all. She worked several jobs and was unable to motivate Eugene to help out or get a job. Instead, she enabled him to continue in his sickness by getting him alcohol, cigarettes or pizza at all hours, whenever he wanted it. She washed and ironed his clothes.

Chrissie's behavior demonstrated codependency by allowing him to remain in this state. She didn't want to keep rescuing him or reinforcing his behavior, but she did. She was trapped by an inability to set appropriate boundaries. Codependency hurt Eugene and it hurt Chrissie. Ironically, when they got divorced, Eugene got better. He biked outside the home, exercised, lost weight and was more open to getting therapy.

A codependent person needs to work on his or her own health and not find meaning in life by always rescuing and saving others even to the point of harming one's health.

Do not date someone so that you can rescue him!

People often stay in a relationship because they think they are called to save the person's life even if it wears them out and drags them down to a point of illness. There is a part of us that thinks this is noble, like a martyr for the cause. The problem with the gift of martyrdom is that you can only use that gift once and then die.

The codependent person always has one more excuse to stay in a bad relationship: "I would break up with him, but he's got a big project at work"; "I would end it, but she is so emotionally fragile that it would crush her"; "I fear what the repercussions will be if I don't do what he asks me to do." The bottom line is always this: "I would end the relationship, but *she (he)* needs *me*." No matter what the damage to self or the relationship, the codependent person keeps the codependency alive and thereby validates his or her existence (or so goes the thinking of a person involved in a codependent relationship).

Be aware that if you have grown up in a codependent family, you are often attracted to repeat that codependency. The man who grew up with an alcoholic mother may seek out a spouse who drinks too much, because he feels wanted by rescuing his wife like he always rescued his mother. Here's the problem: If you have grown up in a codependent family, you might not know it.

You're like a fish that would not know what wet means. To help you identify if you are codependent, look at how your family treats you. Do they make you their sole reason for existence? Look at how you treat your friends. Do you hold on to relationships even if they are harmful to both of you?

Know yourself, and know the person you are marrying. If you have the attitude that says, "True loves means sacrificing all of my needs and wants to rescue someone else," then you may very well stay stuck in that swamp for the rest of your life. If you're thinking, *Isn't that what unconditional love is supposed to be—that you are committed to the other person in want and in plenty, in sorrow and in joy, in sickness and in health?* Yes, that describes marital commitment, but true commitment to your spouse's health does not mean you enable your spouse's weaknesses or illness or addiction to give meaning to your life. A truly loving spouse says, "You need help; get it. And I am not always the one from whom you should get the help you need."

4. Blame Game

If the person you date continually blames you for the things that go wrong in his life, take note. For example, if you happened to unknowingly call at the wrong time while he was writing a business project, and he blames you, watch out. If you choose a restaurant, and she doesn't like it and says you should have known better, beware. Fill in the blank: if the dog bites you and it's your fault; if the dog gets sick and it's your fault; if the soup is too salty or if there is a power failure in the city and you are the one blamed (wow, that would be really weird), quickly get on your horse and get out of Dodge. This person is not the right one for you.

Blaming others indicates a lack of self-esteem—pulling others down to one's own low level to feel good about one's self. Ditto the boss who yells at people or unnecessarily criticizes others. Personal insecurity leads to cutting people below the knees to make them shorter.

Whereas codependency makes you feel like it is your fault and you need to work harder or be more available or be wiser, even at the risk of your own health, people who are good at the blame game believe it's always someone else's fault.

I remember Catherine and Charlie, a dating couple. One day, Catherine went to Charlie's house to bring some food because Charlie was feeling ill. After visiting, when Charlie opened the door to let Catherine out, his dog ran out toward the street. Catherine took off after the dog and at one point was on all fours trying to catch the dog. After tackling the animal, Catherine returned the dog. To her shock, Charlie berated her for letting the dog out. She responded that it was he who opened the door and let the dog out. He told her that if she hadn't come over, he wouldn't have had to open the door and the dog would not have escaped. Definitely the blame game.

5. Parents

You may love the person you are dating, but take a look at his or her parents. The parents give you insight into all the good and bad about the person you might marry. That is why I have couples fill out the inventory in Appendix B before our first premarital counseling session. The inventory includes a big section about their parents' marriages.

For better or for worse, there is an inner script in all of us that uses our parents' marriage as the prime model of married life. It's the main reference point of what works or what we should avoid. Study your boyfriend's (or girlfriend's) parents and the way they relate to one another, for that will give you clues about your romantic other. Know this: If you marry the one you are dating, those parents will also be with you for the rest of your life! They will be involved in one way or another—in how you raise your children and how you will be affirmed or criticized. If they call your loved one every day while you date, they will do that when you are married. If they demonstrate that your significant-other-to-be is their primary reason for living, watch out, codependency may abound. But if they are affirming while demonstrating they know how to distance themselves so that you have your own space, that is fantastic.

Your partner's parents will be with you for a long time. Your spouse might actually become like them because that is the imprint on her or his soul from the time of childhood. You can't change this, but you can prepare yourself for either fun or a hard journey when you meet the parents.

My friend Carl, from Hawaii, was visiting his girlfriend, Louise, on the East Coast. Louise's parents are very prim and proper and dress up for meals at home even on a Saturday morning. (The father wears a tie at home on Saturdays!) Imagine this true-to-life scene: Louise and her parents were at the dining table about to eat breakfast but were waiting for Carl to come out of his bedroom to join them. The parents were conversing, and their backs were to the stairs, which Louise was facing.

At the appointed time, Carl came bounding down the stairs wearing shorts with no shirt or shoes. While this might have been quite appropriate in laid-back and casual Hawaii, here it was very inappropriate. Louise saw Carl first and gave him a horrific look and mouthed with hand motions to get a shirt on and re-dress. Fortunately, Carl ran back upstairs to change before the parents saw him.

Carl got a crash-course insight into Louise's parents and the cultural differences between his and her upbringing. If Carl couldn't adapt, or if this became a point of contention, there would have been a bad virus of division between him and Louise. But he made the adjustment and they have been happily married for decades. (For the record, I consider Carl quite cultured today!)

6. Deception

Deception is one of those viruses that might signal time to immediately pull the plug! If you catch the person you're dating in a lie, you really have to look at it seriously. You cannot base a marriage relationship on dishonesty.

One sad example comes from a couple I married who was outside of our singles group. Within a month the groom had an affair. Within a month! Only in retrospect did the bride realize there had been patterns of deception she had not questioned.

Sin grows in the darkness of deception. It is in hiding that people with addictions find the culture to keep their addictions going. If you catch a loved one telling a little white lie, and then another, it means there is something wrong.

If he tells you he is at one place, but he is really at another . . .

If she said she was given an expensive gift, but then you discover she bought it but didn't want to tell you . . .

If he said he had never had sex with another woman and you discover he actually had sex with three women prior to you . . .

These are all loud and blaring sirens that the person you are dating has some deep issues that need a therapist, not a spouse, to make him more whole.

Carrie and Evan had been dating for about a year. Strangely, Evan did not want to go out publicly for dates. He told Carrie that it was more important that they get to know each other, so it was always best to stay at home. He said, "We have the rest of our lives to be with other people." Carrie's sniffer should have smelled something funny. The only time they went out to restaurants was when they were in a different town.

One day, Carrie dropped off some food at Evan's parents' house because they were sick. When Evan found out later, he was furious. Carrie was confused because she thought she had done a nice thing. It turned out that Evan was dating two other girls at the same time he was dating Carrie. When Carrie found out, all the secrecy made sense. Usually, if someone wants secrecy in your relationship, there is deception involved somehow. Deception is hazardous to your health.

7. Possessiveness

It's not a good thing if your romantic other treats you like he owns you. How do you know if he (or she) is showing unhealthy possessiveness that could suffocate you?

- When he wants to know where you are every moment
- When she gets unfairly jealous if you are out with the guys or someone else, because she feels that you are to be with her and her only

- When he wants to know who calls you
- When she wants to know who writes you personal mail
- When you feel you can't go anywhere alone without your significant other

Jealousy is the belief that a person owns or controls something that is really not his or hers to own or control. Possessiveness and jealousy point to a person's insecurity, low self-esteem, lack of confidence and lack of trust. There is nothing good about possessiveness. Your antivirus soul software should be sending you messages loud and clear that you are walking into a dangerous relationship.

In a healthy marriage, you need to spend time with people other than your spouse. Why? *Because there is no possible way that your spouse will be able to fulfill all of your deepest needs.* Sorry if this is shocking to you. Hollywood may tell you that Prince Charming or Princess Amazing will be your all in all, and you will need no one else. The reality is that other than Jesus Christ, there is no one on earth who can fulfill all your desires, wants and needs. Following Jesus (who is perfect) is hard enough, let alone being married to a sinner who has spent the majority of his or her life without you.

At times your spouse will really bug you. At times you may wonder why you married him or her. At times you may think you should have married someone else. It's to be hoped that these times will pass. But they will only pass in a healthy fashion because you have other healthy, mature friends, in addition to your spouse, who give you perspective, wisdom, encouragement and strength for the journey in ways your spouse could never do. All of your needs cannot be taken care of by one person on earth. Allow other friends to take care of some of your need for friendship, which comes in a multitude of ways. We are such complex people, with so many nuances to our personalities, that one person cannot like all of our hobbies and appreciate all of the arts or movies that we like.

Possessiveness is one of those viruses that does not allow for a healthy community to come around you. As I said earlier, more eyes give clearer vision. We need to have other friends we can socialize with and pray with in addition to a spouse. The counsel of the community is critical.

Cole and Carly had been dating for about six months, but one thing about Cole bothered Carly. He wanted to spend every minute with her. She felt suffocated. She told him that it was important to her to go out with both male and female friends. But he would text her 10 times a day just to ask what she was doing. On a two-hour drive by herself, Carly received four phone calls from Cole. He kept asking, "What's new?" His suffocating behavior made her want to leave the relationship.

Even in marriage, you do not want a spouse who spends every second with you and calls you constantly. Hovering behavior might indicate a lack of boundaries, a sense of possessiveness, a need for control, poor social awareness or insecurity that you might abandon him. None of these are healthy traits.

8. Addictions

If the special person in your life is addicted to alcohol, cocaine, crystal meth, heroin or any other addictive substance, know that though people can pull out of addictions, it is extremely hard to escape. Those who go to Alcoholics Anonymous and have successful sobriety know that on any given day they could slip back in. For many, just knowing that is enough to stay clean and sober. Still, it is not easy. The "a little drink won't hurt" mentality often leads to a lowering of one's guard and a potential journey down the proverbial slippery slope.

A leader in AA told me that once an alcoholic, always an alcoholic—meaning that even when you've been sober for years, you know you can't go back to drinking because alcoholism can resurface quickly. In that sense, if you know you have the alcoholic disease, it is always there, dormant, waiting for the next drink. You can never drink again.

Those who have been addicted to smoking know that for most people it is hard to stop, even with the added knowledge of the danger of secondhand smoke to the family. If they can stop, that is great. But if they can't, the collateral damage of secondhand smoke can't be avoided.

Gambling and pornography are other addictions that will endanger your future.

It is extremely difficult to stop using drugs or stop any other type of addictive behavior. You must be aware of this if you're considering marrying a former or current addict. Look for the signs of health. Look for the signs of denial.

If one has an addictive personality, you have to ask why. Dr. Alan Land has done extensive research on addictive personalities. While no one combination of traits is exclusive, he wrote in a U.S. National Academy of Science Report that addictive personality traits include:

- Impulsive behavior
- A high value on nonconformity with low commitment to goals of society
- Social alienation
- Compulsive behavior
- Heightened stress
- Tolerance for deviant behavior
- Lack of coping skills[2]

Questions to answer: What pain are they trying to anesthetize with drugs or lifestyle? Does the person realize the source of his pain? If not, it's very hard to get healing. Does she know how to resolve the pain other than taking more of the drug? Is it a possible chemical/genetic addiction like alcoholism?

People can turn around from drug addiction, but it's not easy. You need to have your radar up and eyes open if you want to date someone who has an addiction. Can an alcoholic be a good spouse? Yes, if he or she is sober. But if the person gets caught in the web of alcoholism and becomes an out-of-control drinker, your life will land on that slippery slope too.

9. Spiritual Incompatibility

Earlier, I mentioned the danger of spiritual incompatibility. A relationship is usually reduced to the lowest common spiritual denominator. A marriage often descends to the least mature faith. You would think the more mature faith would compensate for the less mature one. But it actually happens the other way around. When the less mature one says, "I don't want to go to church," the more mature one may eventually acquiesce and stop going to church. Even the kids may be affected. It's just too hard to battle it.

Very rarely does the more mature one convince the less mature one to attend worship regularly. The same goes for attending Bible studies, going on a mission trip, volunteering for ministry and tithing. When someone is significantly less spiritually mature than you, it can be like a ball and chain that pulls your faith down.

Are there exceptions? Of course there are. But in my experience of observing parishioners in my church for more than 30 years, it normally plays out that couples move from the more committed to the less committed.

The reality is that if you say Jesus Christ is your best friend, your Lord and Savior, it is really off strategy for a good marriage when you can't share your best friend with a husband or wife. It doesn't help that you don't even have the same perspective on biblical forgiveness, grace, mercy, justice, trust and compassion.

10. Self-centeredness

If you are engaged in a romantic relationship where the other person thinks life is all about him (or her), the relationship will never grow. Narcissism is an egocentric state in which a person thinks life is all about him/her. When you talk about a problem, a narcissistic person responds by turning it to *his* problem. As Bette Milder said in the 1988 movie *Beaches,* "But enough talking about me, let's talk about you . . . what do you think about me?"

Self-centered people:

- Love talking about themselves and move conversations to what interests them or directly to themselves;
- Put their needs before others' needs;
- Feel little or no remorse or guilt about the people they hurt;

- Don't want anyone to criticize them;
- Will hurt you if they feel rejected (or think they are about to be rejected);
- Seek praise by devaluing others;
- Fail to take responsibility for their actions.

Just to be clear: we're not talking about self-interest. It is in your best self-interest to follow God. It is in your self-interest to have a good-paying job. This is different from self-centeredness, which manifests in a belief that the whole universe is about the person (as opposed to about God). It's about serving self, and not others. It's about motivation and action to look good even if it makes you look bad.

11. Lack of Social Awareness

This one is a bit hard to describe. There are some people who are unaware of common relational social cues. I am not talking about etiquette rules like which fork to use at a restaurant. I am talking about people who are on a different wavelength when it comes to connecting with people. If you are dating someone who doesn't get the cultural norms or the social cues, then watch out for that virus, which may bother you for the rest of your (married?) lives.

If you are someone who has a high emotional quotient and social understanding, you will get this section. If you don't, you will be scratching your head. Let's begin with an example of two behaviors, one of which demonstrates a lack of social awareness. On the one hand, you can go up to a complete stranger and ask him for directions if you are lost. Most people would think that is appropriate to do and nonintrusive. On the other hand, if you ask a stranger sitting next to you at a restaurant to have a sample bite of his dinner, you have just demonstrated a supreme lack of social awareness. Here are more common examples of a lack of social awareness:

- Speaking too loudly in environments that dictate other-wise—the library, a nice restaurant, a funeral, and so on;
- Not introducing oneself to others when required;

- Not talking to anyone at a party;
- Not thanking the host upon leaving a party;
- Always talking and not letting others speak;
- Looking at one's feet during a business meeting;
- Smothering/clinging to one's romantic other to the extent that he or she has no personal time.

If you put a value on civility, diplomacy and courtesy, and your date continually violates those values, you might want to opt out of the relationship.

To end this chapter a bit tongue in cheek, beware of people who use horrible Christian pick-up lines. It may show a lack of social awareness. Here are my top ten terrible, awful, pick-up lines that I have either read or heard:

1. You float my ark.
2. For you, I would slay two Goliaths.
3. Is your name Grace, because you are amazing!
4. Now I know why Solomon had 700 wives . . . because he never met you.
5. I didn't believe in predestination until tonight.
6. Hey, I was just reading in the book of Numbers, and I realized I don't have yours.
7. How would you like to join my purpose-driven life?
8. Hey, girl, you know what the temple veil and I have in common? We're both ripped.
9. If I walked around you seven times, would you fall for me?
10. You and me, we're like loaves and fishes; we just might be a miracle together.

Study Questions

1. Have you ever dated a person who exhibited any of the 11 "virus" traits? How would you describe that relationship and its effect on you?

   _____

   _____

   _____

2. After reading this chapter, do you need to take a step back from a current dating relationship or an attraction to someone who may exhibit one of these traits?

   _____

   _____

   _____

3. To which of the 11 viruses named are you most vulnerable?

   _____

   _____

4. Which virus(es) had you never considered as a yellow flag (or even a red flag) behavior?

   _____

   _____

   _____

5. Might you have any of these viruses yourself? If so, what would be the wisest thing to do as soon as possible?

   _____

   _____

   _____

Notes

1. Eric Metcalf, "Are You in a Codependent Relationship?" *WebMD*, April 2011. http://www.webmd.com/sex-relationships/features/signs-of-a-codependent-relationship (accessed December 2013).
2. Dr. Alan Land, U.S. National Academy of Science Report (January 1983).

The Good OS
(Operating System)

Every little action of the common day
makes or unmakes character.

<small>GORDON MACDONALD, *ORDERING YOUR PRIVATE WORLD*</small>

Every computer has a core operating system that runs all of its functions. This chapter looks at the good aspects—the core operating system—of a person that might indicate whether or not he/she is good spouse material. These are qualities to look for and recognize.

Calm in the Heat of Battle

My friends Jody and Eric (with whom I did premarital counseling at Menlo Park) knew they were meant for each other when they both noticed how each stayed focused, positive, compassionate and understanding while everything went wrong during one of their first dates. Neither one panicked. Both remained steady. Steadiness is a good thing.

The following story ranks as one of the most catastrophic dates I have ever heard of, yet it showed the maturity of both people and a kind of street savvy that made them cool under pressure. Here is what happened.

During their first month of dating, Eric was housesitting for some friends who were out of town. He decided to have Jody come over for dinner. As they were preparing dinner, they noticed that Eric's friends' dog, which he was supposed to care for, was sick in the backyard. Though Eric had been warned that the dog was sickly, the dog's illness seemed to have seriously escalated. They quickly put the dog into the host's family car and took off for the family veterinarian.

While at the vet's office, it became clear that the dog would have to be euthanized. Eric had to call his friends and tell them the bad news. Tragic. Losing a family pet is like losing a human family member.

While waiting for the dog to be euthanized, Eric was told he would have to pay the bill immediately. Eric gave his credit card and, for the first time in his life, the card was rejected. Jody, who was just getting to know Eric (and didn't know Eric's friends who owned the dog) had to use her credit card to pay the bill.

They returned to their host's car in the vet's parking lot, and it wouldn't start. Dead. They had to call a roommate for a ride back to the house Eric was housesitting. They went home to finish cooking a dinner that was now hours late.

As they were cooking the chicken, and not fully paying attention, the chicken caught on fire, ruining the dinner. What a "fowl" thing to happen!

But Jody decided to save the night and finish baking her chocolate soufflé. At least they could have dessert, they thought. While mixing the soufflé ingredients, the glass bowl slipped from her hands. As she dropped it, the bowl shattered and the chocolate exploded and flew all over the room and the walls of the kitchen.

It was now late, and they were tired, hungry and had nothing to eat. They had to clean up the entire kitchen of gooey, sticky chocolate, watching for sharp shards of glass. In the end, they still had a romantic (and definitely memorable) evening.

What a night! Sick dog, dead dog, dead credit card, dead car, late dinner, burnt chicken, dessert dropped, dessert exploded, clean the house.

Eric and Jody look back at that night and remember how neither of them lost their cool. Jody noticed how compassionate Eric was with the dying dog, which made her think that he might be good father material. Eric appreciated how steady and calm Jody was during catastrophe after catastrophe, and he filed away in his mind that she might be great spouse material.

All marriages will face tough, traumatic times. People who don't get overly angry and lose their composure, who don't blame others, who can still think straight, who laugh and have a good time, on even the worst date, are a plus for any human operating system.

By the way, Eric and Jody did get married, and it is 23 years as of this writing. In fact, in looking back, Eric said to me, "The requirement of needing to work together, plus the humor of the whole thing, reduced the stress." A time of testing during a date is often more useful than a romantic candlelight dinner for two. A great suggestion for early dating is to go on hikes or a mission trip, or volunteer at a food kitchen to see how your date responds to stress, service and being in the heat of a battle where things go wrong.

Easily Able to Apologize

This is important! It speaks volumes when a person can say, "I'm sorry for what I just did to you." How so? It means the person knows he is flawed. She knows she is not perfect. He is socially aware that sometimes we say things we don't mean and do things we wish we hadn't. The reality is that we make mistakes; we sometimes hurt the people we love the most; we are aware that we have a selfish nature that can fall into self-centeredness and sin.

Saying "I'm sorry" is also the key to a life of bridge building. The key to conflict resolution is to admit when one is wrong, even if it makes one look bad. Saying "I'm sorry" means "I have a lot more to learn about life. I don't have all the answers. I don't even know the right questions. I don't always listen right or speak in a helpful manner. There are so many more chapters to read of how I can improve and that I need to discover more about why and how I tick."

Saying "I'm sorry" is also a powerful expression of humility and an indicator of someone who values the relationship he or she is in.

A True Listener

So much of communication is about listening. We think it is all about talking, but listening is truly the key. Many people when conversing talk a lot because they are basically trying to foist their reality on you. The opposite is that a listener wants to learn. A listener admits she doesn't have all the answers. A listener wants to grow and expand as a person by asking questions for information or clarity. Much can be said for marrying a listener and not a constant talker where you feel minimalized and friends roll their eyes as your spouse tells another unwanted story or opinion.

Often, when my wife and I have gone out to socialize with friends, we have realized later that in a two-hour dinner we might have talked for only about three minutes combined. Here we thought we were invited because they wanted to get to know us. Actually, we were invited so that they could tell us about them—about their adventures, ideas, philosophies and exploits. And so we would just sit there having realized this was not going to be a give-and-take night of an exchange of ideas. And the crazy thing was that often when the dinner was over, our hosts would feel it was the best night ever. Not because we talked—but because they got to assert their reality, their ideas, and had found people who listen well.

I thought maybe Pam and I were the only ones to experience that problem. Then one day, I was reading about the famous director-producer-writer Mike Nichols, who is one of those rare people who has won an Emmy, Grammy, Oscar and Tony Award. That is simply an amazing accomplishment! Imagine his life lessons learned and the adventures he must have had. He is married to Diane Sawyer, nightly anchorwoman for *ABC World News* and previously the co-anchor of *Good Morning America*, anchor of *CBS Morning News* and the first female *60 Minutes* correspondent.

Mike Nichols noted that his wife has traveled all around the world and has met some of the most powerful and interesting people on earth; and yet when they have dinner with people, he is stunned at how few questions his wife is actually asked. Instead, most people prefer to talk about themselves. I think he was humble in saying, "and also no one asked me any questions, either."

Being a former TV news reporter and anchor for the local CBS affiliate in Hawaii, I would love to have a day with Mike and Diane for 10 hours to ask them about their travels, the people they have met, to listen to anecdotes, lessons learned, funny stories and perspectives. I am amazed that others have not seemed interested in who is sitting across the table from them.

But we rarely . . . rarely . . . rarely listen, whether at a dinner table or in a business meeting. We love to talk about ourselves, and why our thoughts and stories are important. So, if you find a person who listens to you, who is interested in you and your stories, grab hold of that man or woman. He or she has a great operating system, which will lead, I bet, to the discovery of many other healthy aspects in that person's life.

In fact, a great conversation catalyst is to ask, "What is your passion in life? What really turns you on?" These types of questions give you tremendous insight to a person.

I would add one more point to listening: As you listen to him (or her) and hear what he has to say, know that most of communication is nonverbal. Observe her body language, eye contact and attentiveness. If the person is constantly looking at his cell phone or texting while on a date with you, he is not really listening well.

Demonstrates Humility

Everyone loves a humble person. So why don't more of us strive to be humble? If you find someone who demonstrates humility as part of his or her foundational operating system, you have struck gold. It is humility that is the incubator for other things like listening, or saying "I'm sorry. I was wrong," or having a teachable spirit, or desiring to serve others and cultivating courtesy.

Humility is a key to health. Why? Because you are healthy if you see life as it really is. Seeing reality can only occur with humility, which allows you to see yourself as you really are. It allows you to know your limits as well as your gifts. Improvement comes with honestly admitting mistakes and learning from them.

Humility is also a sign of high self-esteem. I find that humble people are self-effacing. They don't grab glory, because they know their self-worth and they don't need to flaunt it. They can take jokes and criticism because they have an honest appraisal of themselves. They feel good about themselves and don't care about what people think about them. They also realize their failures are the result of someone else's successes.

They don't take life too seriously. I wear a Mickey Mouse watch every day to remind me not to take myself too seriously. Much of life is Mickey Mouse. But more importantly, I want to have a proper perspective of my words and actions. They're important, but they're not the be-all and end-all of life.

Arrogance is not the opposite of humility, as most people think. *Ignorance* is. Ignorance of how we got to where we are. Ignorance of how little we really know—we are but tiny specks in this gigantic universe. Ignorance of how others—God, family, people—played a role in our success, and how we had a lot of opportunities that gave us our start.

Think about this: Bill Gates was successful largely because he happened to be born into an affluent family and to live next to a university that had a large array of computers, which he could use and learn from. Tiger Woods was successful because he was born and raised in a country that values the sport of hitting a little white ball into small holes. He was also born into a family where he had a father who taught him golf.

Malcolm Gladwell, in his book *Outliers*, points out not only the Bill Gates advantage but also the advantage of hockey players who statistically are more successful mainly because they happened to be born at the right time of the year, which made them older than their counterparts, so they had more months of experience playing hockey when they started out as teenagers. Hence, they were older and more mature and had a lead on the other teen players.

The Bible may say that the husband is the head of the family, but in reality it is a statement of humility! How so? The Bible says the husband must love his wife as Christ loved the Church. "Husbands, love your wives, just as Christ loved the church, and gave himself up for her" (Ephesians 5:25). How did Christ love His Church, also called the Body of Christ? Christ died for the Church. He suffered, was tortured for it. So how does a husband become the head of the household? He has to be the chief servant. He has to be spiritually mature. He has to be willing to suffer for his spouse and children. Too often people say the Bible makes the husband the head, so that means he gets to make all the decisions and lord it over his wife and kids with a "my way or the highway" attitude. He is the commandant, the skipper, the authoritarian. It's actually the complete opposite of those things.

The man should love his wife as Christ loved the Church and gave Himself for it. Therefore, he should be willing to be "crucified" for her and not get his own way. The husband should live to build up his wife and family even it means suffering for him. The husband should serve his wife rather than demand that his wife and kids serve him.

I also think God, in His wisdom, wants the man to be the leader of the family because it is *not natural* for the man to be the spiritual leader. We live in a society where more women go to church than men. Part of the reason is that the Christian life calls for men to be humble, sensitive and compassionate, and those are not our strong points. We like competition and confrontation. We tend to want the external action of doing things, rather than the internal journey of being a spiritual pilgrim/explorer.

There is something about pursuing the spiritual life that doesn't seem to be enough *doing* (too much *being*) for the man. But if God now tells the male he should be the leader, then he has to get serious about his faith and maturity and devotion and commitment to God. And when he does become the leader, it is not from the top down. It means he is the chief servant of the family. He is the maître d' who humbly leads in loving service and sacrifice.

Humility is the key for men and women to grow in faith and in marriage. If the person you are dating is not humble, then I say, *aloha*, and I don't mean hello, but goodbye.

Values Your Opinions

You want a spouse who values hearing your opinions. (Yes, another form of humility!) You want someone who listens because he/she truly believe that God is working through you and sharing His thoughts, and that what you say counts and is valuable, helpful, loving and wise. You don't want a spouse who is more like "Me Tarzan; you Jane." Or even a more derogatory, "I'm the famous Lone Ranger and you are just my sidekick Tonto." People who don't value their spouse's or friends' opinions are truly Lone Rangers. They have walled themselves up. You want a life partner who does not live for every word you say but does value your thoughts.

Oprah Winfrey, in her 2013 Harvard Commencement speech, pointed out that she has done more than 35,000 interviews; and as soon as the camera shuts off, her guests always turn to her to ask, in their own way, "Was that okay?" From President Bush to President Obama, from heroes to housewives, even victims of crimes. "Even Beyonce in all of her Beyonce-ness!" asked after she performed a song, "Was that okay?" Oprah said, "All want to know, 'was that okay? Did you hear me? Do you see me? Did what I say mean anything to you?'"

People want to know they count. They want to know that they are valued as well as their emotions and thoughts. You want a spouse who knows that what you say, what you do, what you think and feel are all important, worth considering and valuable.

Willing to Compromise

Much of marriage is about compromising. When you are single, you can go out when you want to. You can see whatever movie you want to. You can choose the restaurant you want to go to. But when you are married, compromise abounds. I no longer can see the movies or TV shows I want when I want (though it is nice to be able to record it now and see it later when my wife might not want to see it). I can't be as messy as I want to be or as flexible with my time. I hate washing dishes with a passion, but when I got married, I felt it was fair that if my wife was doing the cooking, I should do the cleaning. Sometimes you both are tired, but you know you should do something even though it is more inconvenient for you.

For example, my wife and I got a second dog. I didn't want a second dog. My wife did. But as it turned out, I love our second dog, Molly, as much as our first dog, Max. All is well. People have to be willing to not always insist on getting their way, which also allows for major unexpected blessings.

I have a friend who really didn't want children in his marriage, for five-plus years. But lo and behold, he gave in to his wife and had kids. Now he is so happy and devoted to his children. He can't imagine a life without them! This is the blessing of compromise.

If a person you are dating compromises her desires or his needs in healthy ways, and not in a guilty, codependent or reluctant fashion, that person is a keeper. But again, make sure this is not just happening because you are both in The Weird Zone—when you are infatuated and will do anything for each other. You can only tell if the person truly can compromise if you have "summered and wintered" together for a while.

Exhibits Parent Potential

Here's a great question to ask yourself: *Can I imagine this person I'm dating as the father or mother of my children?* Does he/she exemplify compassion, responsibility, a nurturing nature? Then that is a real plus. It's one of the things you should look for. Now, maybe you are like my friend who didn't want kids. But like my friend, people do change. Should the desire to have children come into play down the road, is your romantic other mature and wise enough to protect you and your (soon to be) family? Can he or she make a positive contribution emotionally, financially, physically and spiritually? If you're not sure how to answer these questions, it might be a cause for deeper reflection before moving forward in your relationship.

Displays a Forgiving Attitude

One of the hardest things to do is to offer and/or seek forgiveness. If you find someone who can do that authentically, then you have someone with a good operating system. To truly forgive does not mean you forgive and forget. I don't think we ever forget, nor do I think God ever forgets. Forgiveness is not condoning a harmful act. It's not excusing a wrong, or saying, "Oh well, boys will be boys," or "Girls will be girls." Forgiveness is not waiting for the one who has hurt you to come to you confessing what he or she did wrong. Sometimes it is as Jesus said: "Father, forgive them; for they *do not know* what they are doing" (Luke 23:34, emphasis added).

Here is what forgiveness is: It is giving up the right to retaliate. It means, whether in thought or in action, I will not desire or move toward retaliation against the other person. Why? Because our perspective on what's fair in terms of revenge/retaliation is so often out of whack. Jesus said, during His Sermon on the Mount recorded in Matthew 5–7, to turn the other cheek (see Matthew 5:38-39), knowing the revenge game always leads to escalation. If someone hits us once, then we will want to hit that person twice. If they come at us with a knife, then we will want to go after them with a gun. If they come at us with a gun, then we want a bazooka, which will lead to a tank and then a drone missile, and on and on it goes.

The Bible says, "Beloved, never avenge yourselves, but leave room for the wrath of God; for it is written, '*Vengeance is mine*, I will repay, says the Lord'" (Romans 12:19, emphasis added). What that means is that we need to get out of the vengeance business because we don't know how to do it right. Let God do what He said: "vengeance is mine." He will know how to do it justly. He has all the facts. He knows everything. If we can trust God to be God, then we can rid ourselves from seeking revenge.

Anyone who understands that, and who can forgive and not seek revenge—that person is platinum! If that person can offer forgiveness to you and seek forgiveness when he or she has done wrong, then God has revealed someone to you of great worth. Anyone who can live out the faith of the Lord's Prayer is invaluable—"forgive us our debts, *as we* forgive our debtors" (Matthew 6:12, emphasis added).

Good at Resolving Conflict

Does he or she have the skills to negotiate an argument in a healthy fashion? Can she effectively do conflict resolution? Know this: You will have arguments in a marriage. You will have conflict. As you are dating this person, do you see signs that this person knows how to move toward resolution when the two of you are far apart on an issue? Does he resort to anger? Does she just pout and go quiet? Does he get passively aggressive? Does she seek retaliation and try to hurt you with words? Is someone going to have a grudge for hours, days or weeks?

I won't spend more time on this one, but I hope you get the picture. Coming to a solution when there is disagreement is a skill that is needed in a healthy marriage. Can you do it? Can she or he do it? If your loved one can build bridges and seek resolution and reconciliation in an argument, this person is probably worth pursuing.

Trustworthy

Is this person's word good? Is there integrity and character behind her or his actions? If this person is trustworthy—where his word is like a bond, or she is a promise keeper not a promise breaker—then you are on to something good.

A strong marriage is based on trust. It is based on knowing that one's yes is yes and one's no is no. If he is a person of trust, it means he doesn't play games. If she is a person of trust, it means you can count on her to be with you when you need her.

Trust is necessary because it helps repair mistakes in the relationship. After one of you blows it, it's easier to trust him when he says, "Okay, I have learned my lesson; I won't do that again." If you can't trust her when she makes that kind of statement, it is not a good sign. But if you've built your relationship on genuine trust in the past, it's easier to trust again. This can lead to a tremendous foundation for a good marriage and family.

Faithfulness is so important in a marriage. You know he or she won't stray. Sometimes your spouse might notice someone of the opposite sex and comment how beautiful or handsome or sexy that person looks. I think that is okay, for that means your "system" still works. God created beauty; God created sexiness. However, as my woman friend said to her husband, "You can read the menu as long as you order the same thing." Meaning, you can look, but always be loyal to me!

Makes and Keeps Friends

Does your partner have friends outside of your relationship? Having a healthy marriage is having a healthy friendship in many ways. You want to have fun with that person, have a great companion for dinner and movies, someone with whom to talk about things. But more importantly, does this person have friends? If she doesn't, her spouse must bear the burden of hearing all the problems, offering all the wisdom and dispensing all of the advice.

If this person does have a healthy number of friendships (in addition to you), then the pressure is off. A healthy marriage needs friendships outside of the marriage for support, encouragement and wisdom. Marriages are always best lived out of a healthy community.

Friendships are also an indicator of your partner's relational experience. If he or she doesn't have a lot of friends, then he or she probably is not experienced in relationships. If she has never had good friends, then your dating relationship will be her laboratory to get stretched in areas of forgiveness, conflict resolution, social awareness, compromise and more. If he has deep friendships with others, then chances are he has great potential for being a good friend and possibly a good spouse for you. As the Bible says, "Iron sharpens iron, and one person sharpens the wits of another" (Proverbs 27:17). Friends take off our rough edges. Friends speak truth into our lives. Friends keep us humble. If the person you're dating tends to break off friendships easily, watch out. You may be next on the list.

Shows Financial Responsibility

Life should not be all about money, but your spouse had better be responsible in making money, saving and investing for the long haul. If your romantic other can't seem to hold a job or doesn't make enough money to support a family, be careful. Remember, once you start dating you either break up or get married. And if you are going to get married, you will want a spouse who has a job that makes a decent living and who understands the value of savings and retirement.

Most people do not even put money aside for retirement.[1] According to a 2011 study of the Life Insurance and Market Research Association (LIMRA), 56 percent of all 18- to 34-year-olds are not saving at all for retirement. When you hit your 20s, only one in three Americans put away money for retirement. You may be really young right now and are thinking, *Retirement! That is so far off! Who cares?* Remember, if you are choosing a spouse who will be with you into your old age, you do have to figure out if this person has the potential to be responsible enough to care for you in the future, rather than be a drag or a financial liability.

Right now more than 9 million senior citizens can't even pay their bills, and 60 percent of older women cannot afford even the most basic expenses, according to two recent studies from the group Wider Opportunities for Women.[2]

In July 2013, the Federal Reserve gave out these statistics:

- Average credit card debt: $15,325
- Average mortgage debt: $147,924
- Average student loan debt: $32,041
- Total American credit card debt: $856 billion
- Average indebted American household owed $17,630

So I hate to say it, but if you are getting serious about someone, you need to know how good they are with credit and savings, or how poor they are in reducing debt. Remember, the above figures are just the *average*. The financial information of the person you are dating might show much higher figures.

According to a recent study by PNC Bank, the average debt burden of a 20-something is $45,000![3] Remember, if you date someone who can't handle a credit card and has a credit line in trouble, guess what? You will inherit that as his or her spouse.

It's understandable how people get into debt—car loans, credit cards, home mortgages. And if you went to college, education debt can be huge. According to a PNC Bank report, 60 percent of Generation Y say they are "really concerned" about their debt. While it's great to be concerned, I'd want to know if they have a plan to get out of debt. When you get married, liabilities are shared.

Her financial weakness is your financial weakness. His Achilles heel becomes your Achilles heel. Then again, his or her savings become your blessings, unless you have a prenuptial agreement.

The problem with prenuptial agreements is that you go into a marriage not trusting the other person enough that you feel the need to build a back door just in case, which can predict trouble. My experience in counseling is that a back door gets built for use. Those who have a prenuptial use it for an eventual divorce. That is just anecdotal, but something to be really careful about.

Why would your spouse-to-be want a prenuptial? Because this is his/her second marriage and he/she needs to set aside things for his/her children? I get that. But if it is because he/she doesn't think the marriage is going to make it, that's bad. Your marriage may already be doomed from day one.

According to a 2009 study by Assistant Professor Jeffrey Dew of Utah State University, one of the best indicators of marital discord is what he terms "financial disagreements." He states that couples who "reported disagreeing about finances once a week were over 30 percent more likely to divorce over time than couples who reported disagreeing about finances a few times per month."[4] Frequent strife about finances is a key indicator of future problems.

Speaks and Acts with Kindness

Kindness goes a long way. It is a precious trait and well worth seeking in someone you would date. Watch how a person treats other people, no matter what stratus of life or profession they are. A kind person is as loving to a janitor as to a CEO.

At the yearly Hawaiian Islands Ministries (HIM) conference, we enlist 35 speakers to teach, some of whom you might even call Christian celebrities—pastors, authors, musicians, Bible teachers, professors and business people. Many would call them godly, spiritual and even Christlike. But we on the HIM staff get to see them behind the scenes. Of course, all of the speakers are kind to me, but I always want to see how they treat my staff and the volunteers. If they talk down to them, they will not be asked back to teach, no matter how eloquently they may speak.

This may shock you, but I have seen people with godly reputations talk condescendingly to my staff and volunteers as if they were slaves. It breaks my heart.

I once heard a pastor say, "That woman is one of the ugliest women I have seen." I was aghast. People say things, when they think no one is around, that give insight into the person they really are. Think about this when you are dating someone. If a pastor whom everyone thinks is gentle and kind proves to be cruel when backs are turned, what kind of person is he really? If the one you are dating seems to have exceptional knowledge, wealth or prestige, do you know the kind of person she really is? Is she genuinely kind and loving to waiters, service station attendants and cashiers at stores? Watch him when he is supposedly talking to the "little people" and see how "big" he really is.

As the apostle Paul wrote, "If I speak in the tongues of mortals and of angels, but do not have love, I am a noisy gong or a clanging cymbal. And if I have prophetic powers, and understand all mysteries and all knowledge, and if I have all faith, so as to remove mountains, but do not have love, I am nothing. If I give away all my possessions, and if I hand over my body so that I may boast, but do not have love, I gain nothing" (1 Corinthians 13:1-3).

Did you read that? You may have prophetic, miraculous powers, be highly knowledgeable and even have incredible faith, but if you have not love, then you gain *nothing!* Talk about a great principle from the Bible to apply to your search for a mate! Your date may be highly accomplished and looked up to and have great knowledge, but if he or she is not kind and loving, that person's accomplishments are no more helpful than a noisy gong or a clanging cymbal.

A Church Attender

If you are a Christian, I strongly encourage you to marry someone who is not just a fan of Jesus, but a real follower. One of the signs of a follower of Christ is whether or not he or she attends church. I don't mean to be legalistic, but if you are truly sold out on God, you worship regularly and are part of God's faith community.

In contrast to being a follower, a fan might say, "I believe in Jesus," but if he or she doesn't really want to praise God or fellowship with His people, something is amiss. If he or she is not committed to spending time each week to totally focus on worshiping God, then something is wrong.

Research by best-selling author Shaunti Feldhahn shows that when you compare people who say they are Christian with those who say they are Christian *and* actually attend church, *the divorce rate drops by 27 percent for the church attenders!*[5] Her new book, *Good News About Marriage*, explains this more fully. In Appendix A you can read more about this statistic and the need for singles ministries in the local church. It does pay to go to church. And you can certainly find nice prospects there. Church attenders are outward focused, involved in service and desirous of hearing a weekly message to help him or her become a better person. What's not to like about that?

Study Questions

1. Which of the operating system traits appeal most to you? Why?

   _____

   _____

   _____

2. Which of the traits are the most troubling?

   _____

   _____

   _____

3. Which traits do you already possess and demonstrate in the way you relate to others?

   _____

   _____

   _____

4. Which trait do you recognize as needing development in you?

_____

_____

_____

5. How could you start practicing that trait today? (Think of a simple type of application, like making sure you listen more during your next conversation.)

_____

_____

_____

Notes

1. Bonnie Kavoussi, "Half of Americans Are Not Saving for Retirement: Report," *The Huffington Post,* May 11, 2012.
2. Ibid.
3. Jillian Berman, "Twenty-Somethings' Debt Burden Averages $45,000, Report Finds," *Huffington Post,* March 22, 2012.
4. Jeffrey Dew, "Bank on It: Thrifty Couples Are the Happiest," The State of Our Unions. http://www.stateofourunions.org/2009/bank_on_it.php (accessed December 2013).
5. Shaunti Feldhahn, *Good News About Marriage* (Colorado Springs, CO: Multnomah Books, releasing May 2014).

Online Dating

Follow your heart, but take your brain with you.

ALFRED ADLER, PSYCHOTHERAPIST

StatisticBrain.com listed the following online dating statistics:

- Total number of single people in the U.S.—54 million
- Total number of people in the U.S. who have tried online dating—40 million
- Total eHarmony members—20 million
- Total Match.com members—15 million
- Average length of courtship for marriages that met online—18.5 months
- Average length of courtship for marriages that met offline—42 months
- Percent of marriages in the last year in which the couple met on a dating site—17%
- Percent of male online dating users—52.4%
- Percent of female online dating users—47.6%[1]

And from the reputable Pew Research Center:

- Reported October 21, 2013 that 11% of American adults have used online dating sites or mobile dating apps.
- 42% of all Americans know an online dater.
- 66% of online daters have gone on a date with someone they met through an online dating site or app.

• 29% of Americans know someone who met a spouse or other long-term partner through online dating.[2]

Who could have guessed that our society would enter a time when online dating is so prolific? But it should be no surprise when considering the short but dramatic increase of Internet use for what we now term "social media." Facebook started in 2004, and today it has more than 1 billion users. Twitter started in 2006 and has grown to more than 500 million users.[3] The 2011 American Time and Use Survey indicates that men now spend 9.65 percent and women spend 6.81 percent of their leisure time online. It should be no surprise to anyone that millions have used online dating.

How do I feel about online dating? I think it is a great option, as long as a person understands its benefits and limitations. Let's take a look at the pros and cons.

Pro: Divorce Decreaser

On June 3, 2013, the Proceedings of the National Academy of Science released a report on a survey of 19,131 respondents. The research showed that more than one-third of those married between 2005 and 2012 met online. The data indicated that when comparing those marriages that began online with those that began through traditional offline venues, the online marriages were slightly less likely to result in a marital break-up—separation or divorce—and they had slightly higher marital satisfaction among those whose respondents remained married.

This might indicate how the Internet is dramatically changing how marriages are created in today's society. But that's not all the report showed. It reported that eHarmony ranked first in creating more online marriages than any other site. What is stunning about the report is that eHarmony not only ranked first in its measures of marital satisfaction, but it also had the lowest rates of divorce and separation of couples that met through other online and offline meeting places.

From 2005 to 2012, of the respondents who were eHarmony subscribers, *only 3.86 percent got separated or divorced.* That is far

below the 20 to 39 percent average (depending on socioeconomics). Granted, online daters tend to be of a higher socioeconomic stratus, which already puts them in the lower divorce rates. But 3.86 percent is very low.

You may say, "Gee, that is a lot lower than your Menlo Park figures. Why is that?" My survey was over a 20-year period, not a 5-year period, which would allow for more separations and divorces. It also doesn't include the so-called seven-year-itch period when marriages tend to go through a difficult time. Nine percent for my Menlo Park figures is actually quite low for a 20-year period.

The report showed that all non-eHarmony online dating services combined had a 6.23 percent separation or divorce rate. So online dating services do help. But also know that when you look at those who met offline in more traditional ways, they only had a 7.67 percent separation or divorce rate. Still low. But that's within the first five years of marriage.

By the way, is there any credence to this so-called seven-year itch where many marriages go through so rough a period they end in divorce? Sociology professor at Johns Hopkins University Andrew Cherlin says, "Most divorces have always occurred within 10 years of marriage because most people who are unhappily married figure that out quickly."[4]

According to an Associated Press article, the Census Bureau indicates (based on 1996 data) that couples that broke up on average separated roughly seven years into marriage. But again, please remember this is "on average." The article pointed out that former Vice President Al Gore divorced after 40 years from his wife, Tipper, and actor/former governor Arnold Schwarzenegger and Maria Shriver separated after 25 years.[5]

The bottom line is that early indications show online dating can be an effective way of finding a spouse for some people.

Pro: Attempts to Find Compatibility

Online dating tries to match couples through compatibility. Sites invite clients to fill out extensive surveys or write essays,

articulating what makes them tick as well as what they are looking for in a mate. That exercise alone is fantastic. It is part of that ruthless self-inventory that helps a person come to terms with what he or she likes, dislikes, is passionate about, is turned on by, and so on. Any exercise that encourages self-exploration is valuable. Some of these online dating services show a real sense of how to create an effective survey.

The online website eHarmony.com was founded by CEO Dr. Neil Warren, a clinical psychologist who worked for more than three decades with married couples, counseling them in happiness and in trauma. It's a big help in finding a spouse to use a company that understands statistical surveys and clinical psychology. I once asked Dr. Warren to speak at one of my ministry events. He is the former Dean of the School of Psychology of Fuller Theological Seminary in Pasadena, California, of which I am a trustee. He taught there while I was a student. His questionnaires are based on his research of the "Key Dimensions of Compatibility." Dr. Warren's vision is similar to mine. He wants to eradicate divorce: "What we're doing is a true social revolution. If you take away divorce and other relational problems, you've taken away one of the greatest challenges that our society has faced. This will change a whole generation and countless other generations to follow."[6]

The website will try to match your core values with another person's similar core values, using a scientific system. That can be really helpful as a resource. Clients get to actually filter out the ones they probably wouldn't like, while filtering in those they might like. All this is done in a protected fashion. That's huge. Prospects can't reach you unless you allow them to.

Pro: Finds People Outside Your Usual Social Circle

It is impossible to survey thousands of people in a short time other than through online dating. The Internet expands the universe of people one would meet through one's usual social encounters. This "expansion of our universe" offers a lot of choices. Normally, our circles of meeting people are the workplace, neighborhood, favorite eating or drinking establishments, relatives, hobbies, church or

community service. But those conditions aren't always conducive to meeting new people who share one's age and life experience. So there have to be other ways to meet people. Today, via technology, we have bigger windows of opportunity.

Pro: Buffet of Choices

Online dating provides a huge buffet of options depending on your interests and background. In addition to eHarmony (one of the first online dating services), other online dating services include:

- Zoosk.com—geared toward boomers
- Match.com—has a large and diverse database
- OurTime.com—focuses on singles over 50
- ChristianMingle.com
- SingleParentMeet.com
- ProfessionalSinglesover40.com
- BlackPeopleMeet.com
- Perfectmatch.com
- Plenty of Fish (pof.com)

I am not endorsing any of the above services, but I list them to show you the industry's diversity. You can limit your search by age, race, religion and interests. It may help you to zero in on what kind of person you are looking for. Within the dating services (like eHarmony.com), you can specify your search into Christian dating, Asian Singles, Black Singles, Hispanic Singles, 30s Singles, and so on. In other services you can search for Jews, Muslims or even farmers!

Indeed, there is quite a buffet amongst these companies. They give you the chance to meet people you may never have been able to meet on your own.

Pro: You Know People Are Interested in Dating

One of the great features of Facebook as highlighted in the movie *Social Network* is the ability to list whether you are available or not.

As my friend Carolyn describes it, "Sometimes at a party, you are hanging out in the late hours talking, but you are not sure if that person is really available or even interested in finding someone." The advantage of an online service is that you know those who subscribe are interested in dating. And that is a big plus in terms of clear communication. Everyone is there for the same reason—they are looking for dates.

Con: Cost

Many online services cost hundreds of dollars. That becomes a deal breaker for many. The Proceedings of the National Academy of Science report showed that their respondents who met their spouse online tended to be from a higher socioeconomic status bracket and were working. This makes sense knowing these services charge fees that one must be able to afford. Though I would say, for a few hundred dollars, if it helps you choose the right spouse, it's worth it.

Con: Takes Time

To be truly honest and authentic, it can take hours to fill out the inventories, questionnaires and forms. If you want something really quick, then online dating might not be for you. On the other hand, this is really not bad, because the more you know about yourself (and the person you might choose to date), the better.

While it may begin as a lot of fun, the process of online dating (and the research that goes along with it) can suck up a lot of time. For some it can almost be like a part-time job if you allow that to happen. Reviewing profiles, evaluating matches, responding to questions and general corresponding—all these have to take place before you may finally go out on a date. That's a lot of emotions and self-analysis, which is not all bad. But it does make the hands of the clock go round and round.

Con: It's in the Writing

If you do not express yourself well through writing, you are at a disadvantage in Internet dating. How you articulate yourself in the survey and in your first email contacts will help a person determine if he/she wants to proceed with you. Poor writing and communication skills may make it much more difficult to find the one you're looking for.

Con: How Did You Meet?

When online dating first started, it carried quite a stigma in the eyes of many. It seemed so artificial. So forced. For some it was as if both God and romance were taken out of the equation. Now, more and more people are finding dates and spouses through online services. And as the research shows, the divorce rate five years in has been quite low. I have seen couples that have used online services in my church who seem to be compatible, happy and are raising their children. Some married couples today still feel embarrassed having to admit they found their spouse online (or are actively searching online for dates). But it is a stigma that has lessened significantly with time.

Con: Appearance Is Not Everything

I know, men all want to date gorgeous women and women want to date guys who have broad shoulders, narrow hips and flat abs. And if you happen to be someone who has the above attributes, you will probably have more inquiries than others. Chances are good, however, that when you finally meet the person you've been communicating with online, he or she will probably not look like the photo. If you have been a person who cares a lot about how people look, I encourage you to spend the time getting to know a person's personality and core values. These are just as important (if not more important) than looks.

My friend Josh told me this story: "A long time ago, I met a girl on Facebook. Her picture was *super* cute, stunning. Then I met her in person and she was unrecognizable. I told a friend of mine about it, and he refused to believe that her picture was that far off reality. So he met her himself. When he returned from their lunch, his only words were: 'That photo was airbrushed by God Himself.'"

Con: Be Careful Out There!

The reality of online dating is that you are sharing a lot of personal information with people you don't know. It is a starting point, but guard yourself. Be careful about what you decide to give out electronically. Once you hit "enter," you can't take it back. Be cautious about going too deep too fast (passing out personal info indiscreetly). Again, until you meet the guy or gal, you won't know if he's normal and stable or a sociopath or pathological liar. And even the last two are hard to determine if the person believes his or her own lies. Again, that is why you need a community to protect you.

According to one report, when it comes to online dating, men lie most about age, height and income. Women lie most about weight, physical build, and age.[7] The report didn't say how many men or women lie, but it says the lies are out there. So beware and be cautious.

Con: Safety

The traditional way of meeting a person "offline" is at a party or other type of function. We can learn so much about another person just by seeing him, by observing her. By the time you say yes to a date, a lot of firsthand information about each other has been acquired. And if you met at a party hosted by a friend, or you at least know the host or someone who knows the host, the host thought enough about them to invite them to the party.

With online dating, you can email and talk on the phone, but it is really hard to evaluate traits like commitment, character, integrity and the like. If a person is self-deceived, he or she may just as easily deceive you. If a person believes his own lies, you may not pick up on it. A person is only as healthy as he truly knows himself. So it is possible that you are about to meet a guy who might hurt you or only want to use you for sex. Hence, I highly suggest always meeting the person in public places and having friends nearby, where they can help you if you need to walk away or escape. I know it makes people feel safe that someone is minutes away by car or at a nearby restaurant in case things get awkward or threatening.

Con: More Exposure, More Flattery, More Rejection

You have the opportunity to meet more people than you would at a party. So while there is more opportunity for success, there is also more possibility for rejection if people don't want to follow up on your picture or your profile or your correspondence.

The fact is, while you are looking at multiple people, the person you are interested in may be looking at multiple people. You have no way of knowing where you stand on the other person's list. But here's the deal with the Internet, and rejection in general: It is an exercise in your sense of self-worth. On one hand it is indeed flattering to receive attention. On the other hand, you have to remember the person doesn't *really* know you. Those compliments are coming from people you really don't know. It's quite common to second-guess oneself and the person communicating with you.

The bottom line is that you can't allow yourself to get hurt over and over again by rejection. As my friend Valerie once said to me:

> I think it's really important in dating, but especially online dating, that one has a healthy sense of self-worth. It can be flattering to receive attention, but sometimes it's not necessarily from the types of people you want it from, and that can make you second-guess yourself. There are millions of reasons for people to not respond, and rejection and non-response is part of the game. You can't take it personally. Also, while online dating works for some people on their first try, it doesn't always work for others; or some end up trying it a few times.

My friend Robin told me the following perspective (and she actually found her husband on an online dating service and is happily married with two young boys):

- Online dating can be brutal on your self-image. At times it is very tough to even get someone to interact with you (no, you don't have to be a supermodel or the tall, dark and handsome CEO of your own corporation, but it can feel like that sometimes).

- You will have to view it like a salesman (or woman) who is cold-calling a client. I have heard that salespeople will get a response from folks (not a positive one, mind you, just a response) just 10 percent of the time. I have found (and others have found as well) that percentage can be about the level you will get someone to interact after you try to approach him or her online or offline.
- Some websites don't give you any idea as to whose accounts are currently active and whose are not. So you might feel badly when someone doesn't respond. But what you don't know is that they gave up online services last year and are *never on*. All you know is that the last five folks never responded. You have to have an excellent opinion of your boundaries and figure it is something with *them*, unless otherwise proven differently.
- No matter how much digital interaction you have with a person via the website, you can only know so much until you get to interact offline. Expect a certain level of "digital rudeness." People can seem interested, exchange emails over several weeks and even say they are about to call—then suddenly break off communication. Don't count any chickens hatching until you have met someone in person. Seriously.
- You do not share any context or community with this person, so they really are a stranger, and you need to interact with them keeping this in mind. Part of what this means is not giving out too much personal information, until they prove worthy. Always think, even humorously, "This person could be an axe murderer!" (Okay, maybe that is a bit too much, but it isn't too much to think this woman could want to swindle you out of money, or this man might want to take advantage of you if he could. So be careful, please!)
- *Go really slow!* Remember, you don't know this other person. You don't have confirmation from others as to who he or she really is over a long period of time. Don't talk marriage until you have dated a year, no matter what your

age. You will save yourself much heartache if you follow this advice. The only case where this rule can or should be broken is if you discover you have people in your life who already know this person and can give a really good and accurate history of the person's character. (This was a huge bonus that I got with my now-husband. We were strangers, but my mom's best friend knew him and his family, as did some of my friends from college, as well as a more recent close friend. I got a really long view of who he was through this history while early in our relationship. But that is a rare thing.)

Which leads to the big question: Does God only have one person in mind for you?

Study Questions

1. What appeals to you about online dating?

_____
_____
_____
_____
_____

2. What are some advantages you were unaware of?

_____
_____
_____
_____

3. What are some of the concerns you had not considered?

_____
_____
_____
_____

4. Why do you think statistics show that marriages from online dating have a shorter courtship period than offline dating, and they show fewer divorces than traditional dating after a marriage of five years?

_____

_____

_____

_____

5. Do you think God has only one person in mind for you? Explain.

_____

_____

_____

_____

Notes

1. "Online Dating Statistics," StatisticBrain.com, June 18, 2013. http://www.statisticbrain.com/online-dating-statistics/ (accessed December 2013). Statistic Brain is a website that specializes in gathering statistics, in terms of percentages, numbers, financials and rankings used Reuters, *Herald News, PC World* and the *Washington Post* for this article.
2. Aaron Smigt and Maeve Duggan, "Online Dating & Relationships," Pew Research Center, October 21, 2013. http://www.pewinternet.org/Reports/2013/Online-Dating/Summary-of-Findings.aspx (accessed December 2013).
3. John T. Cacioppo, Stephanie Cacioppo, Gian C. Gonzaga, Elisabeth L. Ogburn, and Tyler J. VanderWeele, "Marital Satisfaction and Break-ups Differ Across On-line and Off-line Meeting Venues," approved May 1, 2013, by Linda Bartoshuk, University of Florida, as published in the Proceedings of the National Academy of Sciences (PNAS) of the United States of America.
4. "New Census Data Shows That Divorces Are Down But the Theory of the Seven-Year Itch Still Rings True," Daily Mail, May 19, 2011. http://www.dailymail.co.uk/news/article-1388404/New-census-data-shows-divorces-theory-seven-year-itch-rings-true.html (accessed December 2013).
5. Hope Yen, "Census: Divorces Decline but 7-Year Itch Persists," Associated Press, May 18, 2011.
6. Dr. Neil Warren from eHarmony website.
7. "Online Dating Statistics,"StatisticBrain.com, June 18, 2013.

What Does the Bible Say?

I believe the Bible is the best gift God has ever given to man....
All things desirable to men are contained in the Bible.

ABRAHAM LINCOLN

What does the Bible say about finding a spouse? As I mentioned before, the burning questions many singles ask revolve around how to find the right person: Does God only have one person in mind for me? How can I find that one person? If there is only one person, does that mean any other person I date is going to be "the loser"? Or worse yet, what if I marry Person A, and then sometime later I meet Person B, and I think Person B is really God's choice for me?

These are difficult and complex questions. To answer, let me tell a story. It's from the Hebrew Scriptures—what Christians call the Old Testament. Let's see what lessons we can pull from this true story, which is one of the longest of just a few spouse selection passages in the Bible. As you shall see, it grafts in some of the lessons we have already talked about in a beautiful tapestry of truth.

It's found in Genesis 24:1-58:

Now Abraham was old, well advanced in years; and the LORD had blessed Abraham in all things.

Abraham said to his servant, the oldest of his house, who had charge of all that he had, "Put your hand under my thigh and I will make you swear by the LORD, the God of heaven and earth, that you will not get a wife for my son from the daughters of the Canaanites, among whom I live, but will go to my country and to my kindred and get a wife for my son Isaac."

The servant said to him, "Perhaps the woman may not be willing to follow me to this land; must I then take your son back to the land from which you came?"

Abraham said to him, "See to it that you do not take my son back there. The LORD, the God of heaven, who took me from my father's house and from the land of my birth, and who spoke to me and swore to me, 'To your offspring I will give this land,' he will send his angel before you, and you shall take a wife for my son from there. But if the woman is not willing to follow you, then you will be free from this oath of mine; only you must not take my son back there."

So the servant put his hand under the thigh of Abraham his master and swore to him concerning this matter.

Then the servant took ten of his master's camels and departed, taking all kinds of choice gifts from his master; and he set out and went to Aram-naharaim, to the city of Nahor. He made the camels kneel down outside the city by the well of water; it was toward evening, the time when women go out to draw water.

And he said, "O LORD, God of my master Abraham, please grant me success today and show steadfast love to my master Abraham.

"I am standing here by the spring of water, and the daughters of the townspeople are coming out to draw water. Let the girl to whom I shall say, 'Please offer your jar that I may drink,' and who shall say, 'Drink, and I will water your camels'—let her be the one whom you have appointed for your servant Isaac. By this I shall know that you have shown steadfast love to my master."

Before he had finished speaking, there was Rebekah, who was born to Bethuel son of Milcah, the wife of Nahor, Abraham's brother, coming out with her water jar on her shoulder.

The girl was very fair to look upon, a virgin, whom no man had known. She went down to the spring, filled her jar, and came up.

Then the servant ran to meet her and said, "Please let me sip a little water from your jar."

"Drink, my lord," she said, and quickly lowered her jar upon her hand and gave him a drink.

When she had finished giving him a drink, she said, "I will draw for your camels also, until they have finished drinking." So she quickly emptied her jar into the trough and ran again to the well to draw, and she drew for all his camels.

The man gazed at her in silence to learn whether or not the LORD had made his journey successful.

When the camels had finished drinking, the man took a gold nose-ring weighing a half shekel, and two bracelets for her arms weighing ten gold shekels, and said, "Tell me whose daughter you are. Is there room in your father's house for us to spend the night?"

She said to him, "I am the daughter of Bethuel son of Milcah, whom she bore to Nahor." She added, "We have plenty of straw and fodder and a place to spend the night."

The man bowed his head and worshiped the LORD and said, "Blessed be the LORD, the God of my master Abraham, who has not forsaken his steadfast love and his faithfulness toward my master. As for me, the LORD has led me on the way to the house of my master's kin."

Then the girl ran and told her mother's household about these things.

Rebekah had a brother whose name was Laban; and Laban ran out to the man, to the spring.

As soon as he had seen the nose-ring, and the bracelets on his sister's arms, and when he heard the words of his sister Rebekah, "Thus the man spoke to me," he went to the man; and there he was, standing by the camels at the spring.

He said, "Come in, O blessed of the LORD. Why do you stand outside when I have prepared the house and a place for the camels?"

So the man came into the house; and Laban unloaded the camels, and gave him straw and fodder for the camels, and water to wash his feet and the feet of the men who were with him.

Then food was set before him to eat; but he said, "I will not eat until I have told my errand." He said, "Speak on."

So he said, "I am Abraham's servant. The LORD has greatly blessed my master, and he has become wealthy; he has given him flocks and herds, silver and gold, male and female slaves, camels and donkeys. And Sarah my master's wife bore a son to my master when she was old; and he has given him all that he has.

"My master made me swear, saying, 'You shall not take a wife for my son from the daughters of the Canaanites, in whose land I live; but you shall go to my father's house, to my kindred, and get a wife for my son.'

"I said to my master, 'Perhaps the woman will not follow me.'

"But he said to me, 'The LORD, before whom I walk, will send his angel with you and make your way successful. You shall get a wife for my son from my kindred, from my father's house. Then you will be free from my oath, when you come to my kindred; even if they will not give her to you, you will be free from my oath.'

"I came today to the spring, and said, 'O LORD, the God of my master Abraham, if now you will only make successful the way I am going!

'I am standing here by the spring of water; let the young woman who comes out to draw, to whom I shall say, "Please give me a little water from your jar to drink," and who will say to me, "Drink, and I will draw for your camels also"—let her be the woman whom the LORD has appointed for my master's son.'

"Before I had finished speaking in my heart, there was Rebekah coming out with her water jar on her shoulder; and she went down to the spring, and drew. I said to her, 'Please let me drink.'

"She quickly let down her jar from her shoulder, and said, 'Drink, and I will also water your camels.' So I drank, and she also watered the camels.

"Then I asked her, 'Whose daughter are you?' She said, 'The daughter of Bethuel, Nahor's son, whom Milcah bore to him.' So I put the ring on her nose, and the bracelets on her arms.

"Then I bowed my head and worshiped the LORD, and blessed the LORD, the God of my master Abraham, who had led me by the right way to obtain the daughter of my master's kinsman for his son.

"Now then, if you will deal loyally and truly with my master, tell me; and if not, tell me, so that I may turn either to the right hand or to the left."

Then Laban and Bethuel answered, "The thing comes from the LORD; we cannot speak to you anything bad or good. Look, Rebekah is before you, take her and go, and let her be the wife of your master's son, as the LORD has spoken."

When Abraham's servant heard their words, he bowed himself to the ground before the LORD.

And the servant brought out jewelry of silver and of gold, and garments, and gave them to Rebekah; he also gave to her brother and to her mother costly ornaments.

Then he and the men who were with him ate and drank, and they spent the night there. When they rose in the morning, he said, "Send me back to my master."

Her brother and her mother said, "Let the girl remain with us a while, at least ten days; after that she may go."

But he said to them, "Do not delay me, since the LORD has made my journey successful; let me go that I may go to my master."

They said, "We will call the girl, and ask her."

And they called Rebekah, and said to her, "Will you go with this man?" She said, "I will."

What are the lessons we can learn from this account?

LESSON #1

Seek Help from Others

Abraham was humble enough to know that the odds of finding a spouse for his son Isaac were against him. (Sound familiar? And you thought you had it hard with online dating!) So he asked for help. He enlisted the aid of his servant. This is good. It's a form of "it takes a village to find a spouse." The reality is that the odds of our not finding the right spouse are indeed very high. And Abraham had a much smaller surrounding population than we do today. His decision, against astronomical odds, was to affirm that God can (and will) intervene.

LESSON #2

Pray

Abraham was a person of prayer. Prayer should be one of the first things we do when it comes to searching for our future spouse.

So here we have a two-step plan: *Ask God for help. Ask the community for help.* Today that community is friends, relatives, colleagues and, yes, online services. But it begins with the humility of knowing we need help.

Notice that the servant also prayed to God. It wasn't just Abraham's faith and Abraham's prayers. The servant had a prayerful faith too. And what a wonderfully candid, honest and soul-bearing prayer it is: "O Lord, God of my master Abraham, please grant me success today and show steadfast love to my master Abraham" (Genesis 24:12).

The great thing about prayer is that it is not just about your getting the "product" you want; it's not about an end result (in this case, finding a spouse). Prayer is about the process of *you* becoming the right person for marriage. Prayer is about your learning to bask in the presence of God in order to hear His voice and read His signs. The journey is the reward. The process of prayer is the blessing, not just trying to "get someone." The real goal in life, whether as a single or as a married person, should be to draw close to God. Let that be at the foundation of your spouse search. If you really want to find the right spouse for you, you have to pray.

LESSON #3

Base Your Criteria for a Spouse on Character

The servant prayed a very clear prayer with the criteria of what kind of spouse he wanted to find for Isaac: "And he said, 'O LORD, God of my master Abraham, please grant me success today and show steadfast love to my master Abraham. I am standing here by the spring of water, and the daughters of the townspeople are coming out to draw water. Let the girl to whom I shall say, "Please offer your jar that I may drink," and who shall say, "Drink, and I will water your camels"—let her be the one whom you have appointed for your servant Isaac. By this I shall know that you have shown steadfast love to my master'" (Genesis 24:12-14).

I do not believe the servant was asking for any old sign (like "Lead me to a woman who is wearing a blue blouse today"). The servant knew he was looking for both cultural *and* spiritual compatibility. His orders from Abraham were not to find a Caananite woman whose pagan, polytheistic beliefs were in opposition to the monotheistic faith of the Hebrew people. I believe the servant was looking for a sign that revealed a character of servanthood. He was not looking for just any woman. He was looking for a woman who was willing to bring water for thirsty camels—10 camels! That is a lot of trips back and forth from a well to bring water to 10 thirsty camels! In that one request for a sign, he was hoping to find a woman who was courteous, socially aware, had a good work ethic, was not afraid of physical service, was gracious to strangers, and was kind to even a servant. Her kindness blossomed into hospitality when she invited the servant to her home and offered a place to stay, plus food for his camels.

LESSON #4

Know What You Bring to the Table

Often when people look for a spouse, they are focused on what the potential spouse can do for them. "What can I get out of this relationship?" (She makes me laugh, she makes me happy, she knows my needs, and so on.) But what are you bringing to the table? What do you offer to the relationship? The servant made it clear that his master had flocks, herds, silver, gold, slaves, camels and donkeys. This is what Rebekah would get in a marriage with Isaac. (Such a deal!)

A good question to ask yourself is this: When you pray to God, do you find your prayers are focused squarely on you and what you'd like to get out of a relationship? Instead, how might your prayers also include inviting God to reveal (and refine) what you offer to a possible relationship? What are the gifts you bring to a possible future with someone else? As mentioned before, the art of finding a spouse is not finding the right person but *becoming* the right person.

LESSON #5

No Coercion, Only Willing Cooperation

In the end, Rebekah's father asked if she wanted to follow the servant to marry Isaac. That's an amazing thing. In Anicent Near Eastern culture, Rebekah's father could make that decision irrespective of his daughter's desires. But instead he asked her, "And they called Rebekah, and said to her, 'Will you go with this man?' She said, 'I will'" (Genesis 24:58).

No person should be forced into a date or engagement. If it is God's will, the person will join you willingly, not due to trickery or force or persuasion. Not because you cajoled her with flowers and fancy dining. Not because you threw a jealous tantrum. Willingly.

Put all of these lessons together and you have God in the middle of your choice for the best spouse for you. But you say, "You haven't answered the question—is there just one person for me that God has in mind? Or are there, maybe, 50 out there who would fit me, and I just have to find one of them?" In a sense, these are the wrong questions to ask (sorry to disappoint you). First, there are some other questions brought up in this Bible story:

1. Do you trust that if God brought a person into your life, you would know it?
2. Are you praying about a spouse? I mean fervently praying, and not just a once-every-six-months prayer.
3. Do you earnestly desire to grow in your friendship with the Lord, whether or not you find a spouse?
4. Do you have realistic criteria for a spouse? (Note: A good follow-up question is, how do *you* measure up with your own criteria for what a good spouse choice would be?)
5. What do you offer to any potential spouse? Do you have a good job that can contribute to the security of the home? Do you know how to make money, keep a good job and save money? You're going to need all three for a safe future. Do you have the temperament, social skills and character of commitment to make a marriage last?

It does little good to ask if God has one person (or many) chosen for you. That is a smoke screen obscuring the deeper questions listed above. (Remember, I never said finding a spouse would be easy!)

Let's return to my opening paragraph in this chapter. Remember the married-to-Person-A-then-discover-Person-B (who might be "the one") question? I'll close this chapter with a brilliant answer from my friend Jim:

Once you are married to someone, I think that with very few exceptions (adultery, abandonment, serious abuse) God expects you to stick with that person, no matter what. So, your thinking or believing that Person B (and not the Person A you are married to) is somehow God's choice (whether you think that person is a better Christian, holier, more compassionate, or whatever) is really just Satan trying to deceive you at that point.

My feeling is that there is not a single "chosen one" that exists; there are probably a number of people who are right for you in terms of having the basic qualities that could make a successful marriage. The question is, what do you do, and what happens in that relationship once you are married? That is why it is important to have a marriage centered on God, because God will work to bring two people closer to each other if He is in the center.

Study Questions

1. What did the Genesis 24 Bible passage say to you?

_____

_____

_____

_____

_____

_____

2. Which of the five lessons stood out to you as highly applicable to your journey toward marriage?

_____

_____

_____

_____

3. What role do you think faith, prayer and humility play in searching for the right spouse? Explain your answer.

_____

_____

_____

_____

_____

_____

4. Would you be more comfortable thinking there is only one right person as a marriage choice or thinking there could be several right choices? What effect would your answer have on the way you look for a marriage partner?

_____

_____

_____

_____

_____

_____

5. What is the most important takeaway for you from this chapter?

_____

_____

_____

_____

_____

_____

II

Remarriage—Getting Married Again

Marriage is the triumph of imagination over intelligence.
Second marriage is the triumph of hope over experience.

OSCAR WILDE

If you have never been married, you may want to skip this chapter. But if you have been divorced or widowed, and you are thinking of getting married again, this one's for you.

On the other hand, never-been-marrieds, you might marry someone who was divorced or has lost a loved one and this information might be important for you to know some of the challenges and blessings of remarriage.

If you are in the divorced camp, it is not for me to say whether you got divorced for the "right" or the "wrong" reasons. That is up to you. *If you don't know what went wrong the first time, then you will probably bring the same baggage into the second marriage.* Here are some helpful hints for those who get married again after a divorce.

I have already mentioned the value of ruthless self-inventory. If you have gone through a divorce, you really need to know what happened. No divorce occurs because one member of the couple is 100 percent at fault. You really need to know how you might have contributed to the demise of your marriage. Maybe you were too young, or too busy, or you weren't listening. Maybe you had false expectations, or there was a sexual dysfunction. Maybe you weren't committed or completely faithful. Maybe you have an anger or drinking problem. Maybe you are not good at conflict resolution.

Whatever the issues might be, this is a great time as a single to work through some of those and come to grips with how you contributed to the divorce. See a therapist. Talk to a mature, wise friend. God may want to use this time of singleness in your life for self-improvement so that you can emerge a brand-new 2.0 you.

Even those who have never been married should be thinking through why previous relationships haven't worked out (e.g., talk too much and don't listen; bad personal hygiene; pushy; judgmental; and so on). I promise you will repeat the same mistake(s) in the next marriage (or relationship) if you don't figure it out now. What carry-on luggage do you take into relationships? What might you want to leave behind?

As I mentioned before, going through a divorce bears a connection with the zombie film *Night of the Living Dead*. The ex-spouse you don't get along with will still be around. You might have to share the children with him or her and see the person at graduation events and birthdays. There might be unconscious or conscious competition about which parent will give the best present. In a nutshell, there's potential for lots of tension, confusion and awkwardness.

Part of getting ready for a remarriage is to establish as civil a relationship as possible with your ex-spouse and try to make sure you cultivate a forgiving heart. That doesn't mean forgetting the pain and/or betrayal, or condoning how you were abused. Cultivating a forgiving heart results in having no desire for any harm to come to him or her. You need to heal before you are ready for the next marriage.

It was five years before I got married again. It gave me time to think through how I contributed to the demise of my marriage; time to heal from the deep wounds; and time to ensure that I was not going to rebound into a relationship simply because I longed for affection.

Blended Families

If you have kids, and are marrying a person who is divorced and has kids, blending your two families is an issue all by itself. A blended family brings a lot more complexity, tension and challenge to the marriage. You won't be your stepchild's "real" mom or dad. In the eyes of your stepchild, you may be simply "my parent's new spouse." That can be difficult to handle.

Homeostasis is when an environment is in balance. Scientists say that if one element in that environment changes, everything else is affected (and not always in a good way). In Hawaii, mongooses were brought in to kill the rats in the sugar cane fields. But then it was discovered that the cane rat sleeps during the day and the mongoose sleeps at night; so the mongooses were not catching rats. Now Hawaii has thousands of mongooses running around wild—including at my church! Homeostasis in the sugar cane fields got thrown way off due to the introduction of something new.

Take an alligator out of a swamp and the ecosystem changes. Alligators help control the fish, snake and bird populations. Baby alligators are often food for raccoons, crabs, snakes and turtles. During the dry season, alligators dig water holes that offer much-needed hydration for other animals.

Well, you may not be a mongoose or an alligator, but your presence in (and the absence of the former spouse from) a blended family is about to throw off the equilibrium. The homeostasis is off kilter. The environment has radically changed.

Questions to ask yourself and your potential spouse in a blended family scenario:

- What does it mean to your stepkids that the family has you now?
- How will you parent them, discipline them, encourage them?
- How will you financially support them?
- What about college?
- What about the way you write your will?
- Do the stepkids get some of your property after you die?
- Do you want to be rearing children again?
- How will you relate to the grandparents of your stepkids?

There are so many other questions and issues. I have known remarried people who are blessed and happy in their new relationship, but they had to face the issues and know what they were getting into. If you ignore the questions and choose to wait until after you are married to deal with them, then it will be much more difficult for you.

Second Adolescence

After a divorced person goes through the necessary grieving process from divorce, he or she eventually gets stronger and will be ready to date again. My personal belief (after counseling many who have gone through a divorce) is that you wait at least a year after the divorce before you even consider dating again. It takes a long time to process what happened and learn how to become healthy and strong again. You don't want to jump into another relationship because you are lonely or needy. You don't want to rebound into a new relationship because you feel you are incomplete by being alone.

At first, you might find it really awkward to start dating again in your 40s, 50s, 60s—especially if you were married for some time. It may seem like a strange experience, like Tom Hanks in the movie *Big*, where he is a young boy trapped in a grown man's body.

It doesn't matter that you are older; many of those teenage dating insecurities come flooding back. Imagine: You are getting dressed for a date and wondering how you look, where you should take the person out for dinner, what kind of gift you should bring and how awkward it will be during the first kiss if that even happens. You probably haven't felt those uncertainties and emotions for years. And if you have kids, they are not used to you dating (let alone being romantic) with anyone besides their mom or dad whom you've divorced. All of those feelings are normal. It may be a hard transition, but it is all normal, and it is a rite of passage you have to go through if you want to get remarried.

Never take more than your share of the blame, but never avoid the blame if something went wrong.

The final analysis of your divorce and your chance for a new life is to do an honest appraisal of what happened when your marriage failed. Don't take on more than what was truly your fault, but don't escape any admission of your responsibility for what went wrong. In the end, that is what can best prepare you for any future relationship.

Study Questions

1. If you were to list three reasons why your marriage didn't work, what would they be? How did you contribute to each of those three?

   _____

   _____

   _____

   _____

2. How prepared are you for a blended family? What steps can you take to be more prepared?

   _____

   _____

   _____

   _____

3. In what way does the caution of the second adolescence make sense?

   _____

   _____

   _____

   _____

4. What "awkward moments/feelings" have you already encountered?

   _____

   _____

   _____

   _____

5. How are you doing in terms of recognizing your responsibility in the ending of your previous marriage?

   _____

   _____

   _____

Epilogue: God's Grace

Amazing grace, how sweet the sound
that saved a wretch like me . . .

HYMN LYRICS BY JOHN NEWTON (1725–1807)

It is never too late to experience a new beginning with God. This is the first step for the rest of your life. Even if you feel that you've blown it in dating (either sexually, emotionally or otherwise), there still can be a profound, wonderful hope for the future.

As you have read this book, you might have wailed (to yourself), *Oh no, it's too late. I have made some major mistakes. I will never find the right spouse. I already have had sex outside of marriage. I already have lived with someone. I have abandonment issues and serious low self-esteem.*

Know this: God is a God of grace. He always offers you a new chapter to write. He is the Lord of the Infinite Second Chance. Today you can write a new chapter. You can move on because of God's forgiveness and grace. Don't throw a pity party at 2:00 AM. You can change and move on.

The whole point of Jesus telling the parable of the wayward, prodigal son who is forgiven by his father; the accounts of an adulterous woman; of a betraying disciple, Peter; of a doubting disciple, Thomas, who questions Jesus, is that their stories show that we are all given a second chance and are forgiven. The Bible is trying to say over and over again that God's forgiveness is abundant and His love is unconditional. If you decide not to forgive yourself, that is an option; but I personally think it's a really bad option.

- It's never too late to turn around.
- It's never too late to incorporate new ideas into your life.
- It's never too late to have a conversation to see if a relationship is really heading in the right direction.

- It's never too late to accept God's forgiveness and live free.
- God is the God of new beginnings. If by chance you have done some things you wish you hadn't, or that you now realize were unhealthy, then write a new chapter.
- From here on, use the building blocks that make a better foundation.
- From here on, talk to God more about what's on your heart for a spouse.
- From here on, be open to meeting singles in a new, healthy way.
- From here on, focus not on the physical but on getting to know the other person in ways other than sex.
- From here on, get to know yourself, including how you think and why you think as you do.
- From here on, find a community that takes you out of The No Veto Zone.

God loves you. He wants the best for you. If marriage is for you, He wants the very best spouse for you. If marriage is not for you, remember that the Bible calls singleness a gift, because it gives you tremendous freedom and liberty that married people don't have. It saves you from what the apostle Paul calls "anxieties" and "worldly affairs" (1 Corinthians 7:32-33, *RSV*).

As a single, it may mean not having to worry about a spouse, and possibly kids, along with their time demands and living/educational/medical bills, and more. You may feel that singleness is "the gift that no one wants." But it is a gift to go all out for God in ways others cannot. You have more flexibility to travel, have fun, experiment and live life to the fullest.

For those who really want to get married, remember the blessing and the process of waiting and following these principles. When I got married the first time, at age 21, I didn't know Pam, for she is 7 years younger. That would have made her 14! Obviously, I did not date her then. God's plan was that I wait many years for the partner He wanted me to have. When I got divorced it was 5 more years of singleness for me. I met Pam when I was 29. I married her when I was 30.

Pam and I both have an entrepreneurial spirit willing to risk for God and give a lot of our money away. We have the same kind of humor and similar interests in ministry and movies! She is a phenomenal mother who raised three wonderful kids who all love Jesus. She has high integrity and character. She is a great cook!

But I had to wait another five years after my divorce for the one God had in mind for me. In retrospect, when I was 21, I should have waited 9 years more instead of getting married to the one who wasn't the right fit for me. So if you are single, I know it is hard to hear that you need to wait for the right person, but it is worth waiting for—no matter how long the wait!

Whatever age you are now, take the time to choose wisely. Be patient, and remember this promise from God:

Do not fear, for I am with you, do not be afraid, for I am your God. I will strengthen you, I will help you, I will uphold you with my victorious right hand (Isaiah 41:10).

God bless you.

Appendix A

A Plea for Churches to Have a Singles Ministry

*By this everyone will know that you are my disciples,
if you have love for one another.*

JOHN 13:35

There are compelling reasons for a church to have a singles ministry. The lessons I learned from a successful singles ministry, which is why I wrote this book, can be duplicated.

While 44 percent of the adult population (18 years and older) of the United States is single (see census.gov), most churches all but ignore this significant part of the population. That amounted to 102 million single people in 2011. Churches might have a children's ministry, a youth ministry and maybe a men's or women's ministry. However, there is a tendency for churches to ignore singles, to subtly despise divorcé(e)s as failures or losers, or to not know what to do with widows/widowers.

Churches expect singles to get married and often only have programs for married people with kids. There is little in-between teaching for singles prior to marriage. Sermon illustrations, more often than not, center around having a spouse and kids.

Yet, singles have specific needs. If churches had a staff person and a ministry emphasis toward singles, there could be much prevention of heartache and an increased chance of a fulfilled life. Good principles on love, sex and dating would enhance the chance of having happier marriages and fewer divorces. Those who are in pain (widows/widowers, divorcé[e]s, lonely singles) would find specific community and teaching to help them.

Churches often bewail abortion, AIDS, homosexuality and divorce in their communities, but by not having a singles ministry, they miss out on doing important preventive and care-giving work that singles so desperately need.

When I had the blessing and the challenge of starting a singles ministry department at Menlo Park Presbyterian Church, the church took a gamble in terms of money and staff. It was a gamble well worth it because it was clearly led by the Holy Spirit. Within three years we had thousands of singles on our mailing list and eventually had more than 700 in a regular singles ministry, not including the many social events happening every week.

First of all, let's bust a myth. You and I have heard many times that the divorce rate for Christians and non-Christians is the same. The same goes for extramarital affairs. But in all research, you have to really look at how the questions are asked. *What defines being a Christian? Is that Christian really a follower of Christ or just a fan who applauds from the stands? Does the Christian even go to church, which might be an indicator of a true follower of God?*

If you attend church regularly, the divorce rate dramatically decreases! Best-selling author Shaunti Feldhahn, whose book *For Women Only: What You Need to Know About the Inner Lives of Men*, published in 2004 and revised and updated in 2012, has sold more than 1 million copies in 15 languages. She challenged the research that said the divorce rate is the same for Christians and non-Christians. In her latest book, *Good News About Marriage*, she discovered that the early research interpretation was flawed because it compared non-Christians with people who "claimed" to be Christian. When she did her own research analysis and asked to compare those who claimed to be Christian with those who had actually attended church in the last seven days (from those who had not), *she found that the divorce rate drops by 27 percent!*

Feldhahn reported, "Contrary to popular belief, going to church *does* make a huge difference not only for those married but also, as my survey shows, for those who are single in having a marriage that can last a lifetime!"[1] Hence, finding a spouse who is already a church-goer dramatically increases your chances for a lifelong marriage.

For years, many churches have spoken out against homosexuality, but rarely does one find a church that has a major ministry helping homosexuals become accepted in society and not abused in school or in the workplace. For years, churches have spoken out against abortion, but rarely does one find a church that has a major ministry in helping pregnant moms think through their options. Churches may speak out against divorce yet what do they really do for singles to help them find a mate and learn healthy principles of having a lifelong marriage? The Bible speaks plainly about helping the widows, but how many churches have a ministry specifically for the widow and widower and *their* needs?

Forty-four percent of the population is single. That's a huge percentage of people who need a ministry geared toward them. That's 102 million singles over the age of 18. The *Harvard Business Review* reported in 2012 that the number of single people in America is growing at more than *twice* the rate of those who are wed; and if the trend continues, there soon will be more single adults than married adults in the U.S.[2]

If a church helps people prevent a divorce, imagine the heartache that could be avoided. If a church helps singles to keep from getting into unwanted pregnancies, that is a major detour away from unnecessary pain. If a church helps those who have lost a spouse through death cope with the loneliness, depression and feelings of helplessness, that is fulfilling the Bible's mandate to help the widows:

> If any believing woman has relatives who are really widows,
> let her assist them; let the church not be burdened, so that
> it can assist those who are real widows (1 Timothy 5:16).

> Honor widows who are really widows (1 Timothy 5:3).

> Religion that is pure and undefiled before God, the Father,
> is this: to care for orphans and widows in their distress,
> and to keep oneself unstained by the world (James 1:27).

In judgment of those who care not for widows, Scripture says:

> Your princes are rebels and companions of thieves. Every-
> one loves a bribe and runs after gifts. They do not defend

the orphan, and the widow's cause does not come before them (Isaiah 1:23).

I would add that there can be a bias in churches against senior citizens because they are old and, often, are not in power and have no advocates on policy-making boards. And if they are widows or widowers, it is much harder. But the Lord God Himself said we need to honor them and take care of them: "Stand up in the presence of the aged, show respect for the elderly and revere your God. I am the LORD" (Leviticus 19:32, *TNIV*).

According to America's Families and Living Arrangements, in 2011, of those who claimed to be single, 62 percent of unmarried U.S. residents 18 years and older had never been married; 24 percent were divorced; and 14 percent were widowed. There is tremendous need for a ministry to singles. To be sure, it is very difficult to start a singles ministry because you need to find a leader who is gifted in compassion, administration, teaching and has a proven record in entrepreneurialism in starting a ministry from scratch.

My church presently doesn't have an all-encompassing ministry for singles of all ages. We have searched for a leader but have not found the right one. We have tried out several pastors, but it was not the right fit. It is not an easy job description. It is almost like finding a senior pastor for a subgroup of the church that could explode upward in numbers if guided properly. We do, however, have an ongoing singles ministry for "older singles" (60+ years of age). They have a weekly Bible study and social events that attract between 60 and 80 people. We also have a great divorce recovery ministry and a group for those who have lost loved ones through death.

If you can find a gifted and charismatic leader who has a heart for people of all ages who have never married, or who are divorced or widowed, you will be amazed by how hundreds if not thousands will flock to your church. Singles are looking for a safe alternative to bars or clubs, where they can find real community and a leader who will love, support and equip them in life.

Singles are looking for a place where there is a critical core of people, and where it will be fun and healthy. Singles are looking for a place where they can serve with others. Singles are looking for principles of living. Singles are looking for a place that is not a *meat* market, but instead a place to *meet* people. Christian singles are looking for other Christian singles, and where better than a church? Christians are looking for a community that is relatively safe from those who just want a sex partner. Remember, 44 percent of the population is single. It's a huge market opportunity.

At one point at Menlo Park Presbyterian Church, where I served as singles pastor, there were more singles members than married members in the 3,000+ membership. You build a healthy singles ministry and they will come. I could write an entire book on how to start a singles ministry. But here is a real quick list of tips for starting one.

STEP ONE

Staff Leadership

Finding a pastor or staff person who has the leadership gifts required to build a ministry is so very important. I would suggest looking for a man, because contrary to popular belief, men come where there are a lot of other men, not where there are a lot of women. If a man comes to a group that is predominantly women, he's not likely to stay. Most singles groups have a high percentage of women. To counterbalance that, it is good to have strong, male leadership. Both the men and women will appreciate it. At Menlo Park, I led my singles ministries with a woman. That was good, because it gave helpful options for counseling. But I would strongly encourage having male leadership for singles ministry organizations and events.

This staff person must be a good upfront teacher; have a high emotional quotient and social skills; have a merciful heart for dealing with those who have lost loved ones, either through death, divorce or broken relationships, and with those who suffer from loneliness. You also need a leader of the highest moral caliber. It will ruin your ministry if the leader falls to an affair or even has an appearance of impropriety. Dealing with singles all the time means one needs healthy boundaries for ministry.

There also needs to be complete buy-in from the senior pastor. He or she needs to fully back the staff person in charge of singles and the singles ministry itself. The ministry can't be an oversight or a stepchild. Just as most senior pastors fully encourage children's, youth, men's or women's ministries, so too the senior pastor must completely back a singles ministry. It is counterintuitive since there is such a heavy bias toward married people, but it is nevertheless crucial.

STEP TWO

Understand Singles' Needs

There has been a stigma against singles that results in their being treated like second-class citizens (as seen in the lack of conferences, seminars and church departments created for them). But the Bible says so clearly in 1 Corinthians 7:28 that if you are single, remain that way because it would spare you "troubles, emotional distress or worldly anxieties" (depending on the translation). Hence, I would make a biblical case that being single actually makes you "first class." If you can't handle being single, then move on to "second class" and get married, for you now enter into a life with more "troubles, emotional distress and anxieties"! The Bible is often upside down compared to how we think (turn the other cheek; if he asks for your coat, give him your cloak too; forgive and love your enemies; and more), and this area of single versus married is another case.

Being a "first-class single person" comes with a lot of specific issues the church can help equip one to deal with (e.g., loneliness, spouse selection, temptation to have sex, dating guidelines, grief recovery from breakups, social awareness). I mention social awareness because some are single for a reason—they don't easily get along with others.

Singles live in a church world where they can feel like second-class citizens. If you have never been married, people may wonder, *What is wrong with you?* If you are divorced, they may think you are a loser who can't keep a husband or wife. In some churches, they may think you are a sinner who "got what you deserved" by not staying in your marriage. If you are a widow or widower, not everyone knows how to help a person who has lost a spouse. They don't know what to do or say.

Especially in church, we hold up the nuclear family of a mom, dad and children as the only viable model. But singles have a calling from God just like everyone else. Singles need a staff leader who will be a champion for them. Find someone who will defend and speak for those singles. Singles are also rarely on the church's highest governing boards, so it can become a case of "out of sight, out of mind." Scripture reminds us, "Take care of any widow who has no one else to care for her" (1 Timothy 5:3).

STEP THREE

Lay Leadership

There is a reason Jesus prayed all night before choosing the 12 disciples (and even then, one of them eventually betrayed Him). After finding a staff leader, the leader's greatest job is picking who will comprise the lay leadership team for the Singles Ministry. This is critical. This is the biggest decision of the ministry. It's difficult to find healthy, humble, spiritually mature singles with high social skills. (Coincidentally, it's just as hard to find married people with the same qualifications.) However, with the tendency for singles to have a "bruised" nature—rejected, divorced, grieving—it can be harder.

When I first came to my church as a singles minister, a significant number of the lay leaders were sleeping with one another. They were a flock without a shepherd. Many of them may not have known Jesus as friend and Lord. On their own they did pretty well in terms of organizing. The older singles (40+ years old) already had about 100 people in a weekly meeting. That attendance alone showed how big a need there was.

When my current church holds a singles social event, 60 will show up (and that is without staff help). When I was at Menlo Park Presbyterian Church, the younger adults (20s and 30s) had about 35 to 50 meeting, with two great elders of the church who led a Bible study with them. But they all needed a shepherd to equip, nurture and recruit leaders.

Eventually, we had two major singles groups: (1) those above 40 years of age and (2) those below 40 years of age. I had 12 leaders for each group. Two leaders were assigned to one of six areas:

1. Spiritual Life: in charge of Sunday morning or evening study/fellowship time and running our retreats (which could have 200 to 300 people)
2. Communication: in charge of maintaining the mailing lists (that had grown from 1,000 to 1,500 in each of the groups and would change up to 50 percent every six months)
3. Small Groups: we had a strong small-group ministry that would meet during midweek, though the younger singles would meet on Sunday night after I taught.
4. Social: which led to roughly six social events per week! Potlucks, dances, hikes, weekly volleyball games, theme nights, and more
5. Outreach: Finding service opportunities to help the oppressed or the needy
6. Prayer: an essential part of our singles ministry (if a ministry is not undergirded with prayer, then forget it)

There was also a special group of leaders for Divorce Recovery. Every Monday night an ongoing group of people who had been divorced received tremendous care and feeding.

It was important that all of my leaders were single themselves. I felt strongly that it would be condescending for married people to lead our singles ministry. Single adults are adults.

Let them run it. Yes, I was the staff person, and I was married. But the fact that I had been divorced really helped.

I remember when I first talked to the older singles. There were about 100 people present. It was my first introduction to that group. Very early on in the meeting a man in the back, named Chuck, raised his hand to ask a question that was chilling, to say the least. He asked, "What right do you have to become our pastor? You come here to California. You are from Hawaii. You are married, with a child on the way. How can you possibly know what it is like for us who have suffered the pain of divorce or the loss of a loved one?"

Ugh! Great start for me.

And so I replied, "Uh, I was divorced." I told my story.

There was an awkward silence.

Then Chuck said, "Well, then, welcome aboard!"

I realized that as horrible as my divorce was, it was also going to be used for good. Satan had wanted it to be used for evil, but now it would be used for good. I was reminded of Henri Nouwen, who coined the phrase "wounded healer." That was me. I would come alongside them, not from on top or beneath them. I was wounded as they were wounded. And like a beggar helping another beggar, we would find the Bread of Life together. As their pastor, they knew I would feel their pain, embarrassment and hopelessness. I wasn't above them. I was with them, alongside them. I was once there. I was once depressed and blinded by despair. But I could also say with validity, "I once was blind, but now I see."

Every month I would have the leadership group over to my house for dinner at 6:00 PM. It was always potluck dinner, and we would visit and check in with each other. And then around 7:00 PM, we would take two hours to go over the logistics of running a ministry. For me, those monthly meetings with each of the two groups were priceless. We laughed; we supported one another; we planned and strategized. Many of those leaders today are still good friends, and many of them still support me and even work with me in ministries together (yes, decades later). Some lead their own ministries, literally all over the world.

I would consider the days of my being a singles pastor one of my most memorable experiences. It was the high point of my entire ministry at Menlo Park. I had to leave that ministry and church because my father died unexpectedly. I returned to Hawaii to take care of my mom (a new widow). If it were not for something as catastrophic as that, I probably would have stayed for many more years as a singles pastor. People who serve as singles pastors will find it challenging but incredibly fulfilling.

STEP FOUR

The 3 Ss

It is easy for a singles ministry to become just a big social time. That is what singles gravitate toward, especially at the beginning. Think of an equilateral triangle in ministry. Each side is important for true equilibrium. Without one of the sides, your ministry becomes obtuse. It is like a tricycle with one wheel off. It just won't work. It won't be healthy.

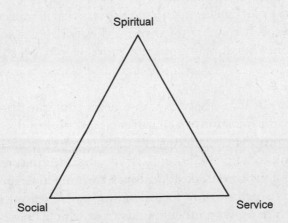

There has to always be a balance between three elements: spiritual, social, service.

1. Spiritual

Clearly, a ministry is about helping people find friendship and lordship with Jesus Christ. He is the ultimate "partner for life." Stray away from that and the group becomes a singles get-together for fun (and maybe some pop psychology self-help principles). Teaching them principles from the Bible for living as a single is the best well-worn, time-tested stuff of which a good, fulfilled life is made. The bottom line is that many people will come, so you have to remember *why* you are there. And that is to lead people into the healthiest life of all. For a church, and for many recovery groups, that is through Jesus Christ.

When someone has a broken arm, it is important to put the arm in a cast so that it will mend properly. When someone experiences a rejection, a breakup, a divorce or a death in their life, it is vitally important to guide him or her to put on the "cast of Christ" (and His principles for living) and then, as doctors tell us, at the place of the break it will become stronger than ever.

2. Social

Yes, singles want social events—many of them. A buffet of events will cater to people who are athletic or like dancing or like to eat or just talk. Have a menu of events that will appeal to the athletic, the introvert, the extrovert, the artistic, the academic, and so on. The more options, the more people will come.

3. Service

If you do not have a service component, your ministry will be ingrown, provincial and insular. It can only think of itself, which is not healthy. The best ministries have a strong service element. Find ways to help the poor, both locally and internationally. Find mission projects like food drives, tutoring underprivileged children (which was big for us), community clean-up events, and the like. Serving others builds friendship as people work alongside each other. Sometimes serving is better than being at a dance (which can actually be quite nerve-wracking, and brings back a lot of bad high school memories!). But a service project, where together you are making a difference in the world around you, is helpful in so many ways.

Additional tips on running a singles ministry:

- Young adults will not want to be referred to as "singles," while older adults usually do not mind. Be aware of this when you name your ministry.
- Men will attract other men and women. Women tend to attract other women. Strange, huh? If you have a lot of women, men will probably not come. You would think they would see it as a target-rich environment, but it is actually a turnoff to men. Men come when they see other men present (and in numbers).
- The healthier the leadership, the healthier the group.
- If you are the staff leader, you do not have to go to all the social events. It will wipe you out.
- You *must* have the endorsement and enthusiasm of your senior pastor to launch a singles ministry. When he mentions it from the pulpit, when she endorses it in the budget meetings, when he encourages you when you are down, it is critically important.
- You must have a budget for a singles ministry. Like youth ministries, you will have retreats; you will need money for food and socials; you will need money for entertainment and meeting with leaders, members and prospective members for meals.
- Maintain healthy personal boundaries. No nighttime counseling. Only do counseling if your staff is around. If married, let your spouse know if you are having a meeting with the opposite sex for coffee or a meal. Don't burn out; singles, like most people, will love to talk and can take up a lot of time in counseling or at meals. Also, many of the issues singles deal with are sad (due to their grief, rejection and the compounded problems of raising children in a blended family). Prepare yourself emotionally for this. You need to take time to regroup and refresh.

Special Projects

A special service project can bring in tons of people into your church. I remember the late Bill Flanagan, a pioneer of singles ministries, who started a large singles ministry at St. Andrews Presbyterian Church, in Newport Beach, California. He created a multi-week divorce recovery series that dealt with grieving, loneliness, depression, dating, choosing a spouse. He would use Bible stories to teach those principles.

But what was creative about the series was that Bill would promote not only at his church but also in the community. He made friendships with key judges and attorneys and would send his brochures to the family courts and divorce lawyers, advertising his series two or three times a year. I remember Bill telling me that he would get 150+ people attending—most of them unchurched! It was through his divorce recovery series that people would find hope, tools to cope, and maybe a church home. Much of the church growth in that church was due to his divorce recovery ministry.

Of the many ministries I have led or taught in churches, Divorce Recovery was/is clearly one of my favorites. Why? There are no masks in Divorce Recovery groups. Everyone knows why they are there. They all have a hurt. They all want help. They all need friends. They all desire some tools to help them cope and heal. When there is that authenticity and transparency, a lot can get done and the love quotient rises in this environment of humility and openness.

It is like an Alcoholics Anonymous (AA) meeting where everyone is there for the same reason. There are no masks and no hiding. All admit their weakness and desire for growth. It's the same for Divorce Recovery. Starting a Singles Ministry is a big commitment for a church, but it really works.

Earlier, I mentioned the best-selling author Shaunti Feldhahn. What I didn't say is that she found her spouse through a church singles group. Here is what she wrote and wants to share with you:

> One of the reasons I have a great marriage—and that I've
> spent the last 10 years working to encourage and help

the marriages of others!—is due to the type of absolutely foundational teaching found in this book.

For the three years between college and graduate school, I attended a large church that was quite similar to Menlo Park Presbyterian where Dan Chun was the singles pastor, championing a very important and strategic approach to friendships, dating, choosing a spouse and premarital counseling. In fact, my singles pastor eventually ended up at Menlo Park after Dan left, continuing the same theme of teaching. And what I can tell you with certainty—having witnessed it in my own life and in the lives of dozens of friends who met and married through my own church's singles ministry—is that this teaching works.

The message is not just about which spouse to pick, but how. Not just about principles that will make all the difference in friendships and dating, but about laying the right foundation for an eventual marriage. And in a culture with far too many divorces, this preparatory work acts like an inoculation against so many ills that often damage our marriages. As you will see in this book, the marriages launched via this teaching have an amazing success rate compared to the national average.

When I was an active participant in that singles ministry 20 years ago, many churches had similar approaches. For some reason though, today, many of those singles ministries no longer exist in the same way—or don't exist at all. I think we need them back! Today, many churches with large swaths of singles have switched to focusing primarily on building character and relationship with God, rather than on providing intentional guidance and a safe forum for building healthy, strategic relationships with one another—including dating relationships. I know churches are legitimately concerned about not turning houses of worship into "meat markets." But having experienced the gift of a well-thought-out singles ministry that actively provided opportunities to meet other singles, I know firsthand just how vital it is.

Our ministry, like Dan's, created excellent boundaries within which people were safe to grow in their relationship with God *and* meet other singles who shared their most important values—and then be led through the process of evaluating whether a particular friendship could or should turn into something more.

That type of involved, ultra-intentional singles ministry is a rarity these days, but we need it now more than ever. And Dan Chun has a passion to lead that charge. Men and women—whether young singles, or single again—need a firm foundation of more than just their own relationship with God and their own character; they need fellowship with others who are walking the same road (both those of their own gender *and* those of the opposite sex), wise counsel, solid principles on which to evaluate their relationships, a mentor to walk the road with them, boundaries to follow and accountability. While the first and last needs can only be met in the context of an involved singles ministry, I'm thrilled that Dan is capturing the rest in a book that guides those who don't have the benefit of one. I'm also thrilled that this will be an opportunity to lead the charge for our culture—especially within the Christian community—to be more strategic about launching our singles into relationships well.

I benefited from that, and everything in my life is different as a result. I know every reader of this book will feel the same.[3]

Notes
1. Shaunti Feldhahn, *Good News About Marriage* (Colorado Springs, CO: Multnomah Books, releasing May 2014).
2. Annalyn Censky, "Why the Jobs Recovery Favors Single Workers" *Harvard Business Review, The Daily State,* CNN Money, August 21, 2012.
3. Shaunti Feldhahn is a social researcher, national speaker and best-selling author of *For Women Only: What You Need to Know About the Inner Lives of Men* (which is in the top 1,800 of all-time Amazon.com book sellers) and *For Men Only: A Straightforward Guide to the Inner Lives of Women.*

Appendix B

Premarital Information Form

Today's date _____ Wedding date _____

Personal History

General Information
Name _____ Birthdate _____ Age ____
Address _____
City _____ State & zip _____
Phone numbers
Cell _____ Home _____ Work _____

Permanent Address After Wedding
Address _____
City _____ State & zip _____

Marital Status
Never been married _____ Widowed _____ Separated _____
Date of separation _____
Reason:

_____
_____
_____

Divorced _____ # of times _____ Date(s) _____
Reason:

_____
_____
_____
_____

Children

Name_____Age_____
Residing in _____
Name_____Age_____
Residing in _____
Name_____Age_____
Residing in _____
Name_____Age_____
Residing in _____

Work

Occupation _____
Name of employer _____ Years in the job _____

Education

Last year completed _____Degree/diploma_____
Major (if college) _____
School_____
Other type(s) of training:

_____
_____
_____

Military Service

Branch_____ Number of years_____

Health Status

Your general health is Very Good __ Good __ Average __ Poor __

Describe important present or past illnesses and handicaps:

_____
_____
_____

When was your last physical exam? _____
Results_____
_____

Have you ever been under treatment for emotional problems?
Yes _____ No _____
If yes, describe when, why, and under whose care:

_____

_____

_____

Have you ever used, or are you using, agents that may induce
chemical dependency?
Yes _____ No _____
If yes, what drug have you used or are you using?

_____

_____

_____

Have you ever been arrested? Yes ____ No ____
If yes, explain:

_____

_____

_____

Personal Attributes
Describe yourself in terms of personal characteristics:
a) Positive traits

_____

_____

b) Negative traits

_____

_____

Describe the worst thing that ever happened to you:

_____

_____

_____

_____

_____

_____

Describe the best thing that ever happened to you:

_____

_____

_____

_____

_____

Describe the person who had the greatest influence on your life:

_____

_____

_____

Christian Perspective

Are you a Christian? Yes _____ No _____

If no, why do you desire a church wedding or minister?

_____

_____

_____

_____

Define what a Christian is:

_____

_____

_____

_____

What role do you expect your faith to have in your marriage?

_____

_____

_____

_____

How has God guided your decision to marry?

_____

_____

_____

_____

Family History

Father's name _____

Living or deceased? _____ Age _____

Father's residence

Address _____

City _____ State & zip _____

Father's occupation _____

Highest education level completed _____

Father's current marital status

Married _____ Separated _____ Divorced _____ Widowed _____

Has your father ever been:

Separated _____ Divorced _____ Widowed _____

Mother's name _____ + _____

Living or deceased? _____ Age _____

Mother's residence

Address _____

City _____ State & zip _____

Mother's occupation _____

Highest education level completed _____

Mother's current marital status

Married _____ Separated _____ Divorced _____ Widowed _____

Has your mother ever been:

Separated _____ Divorced _____ Widowed _____

Father's character traits:

a) Positive traits

_____

_____

b) Negative traits

_____

_____

Mother's character traits:
a) Positive traits

_____

_____

b) Negative traits

_____

_____

Describe what you've observed in the following areas of your parents' relationship:

Friendship/companionship/frequency of being together:

_____

_____

_____

_____

Intensity of relationship (competitive, combative, cool, casual, affectionate, romantic, and so on):

_____

_____

_____

Decision-making/leadership roles (who led and in what ways):

_____

_____

_____

Religious training in the home (who trained and how):

_____

_____

_____

Management of finances (who managed the money; what did they do with the money; how successful were they in this task):
_____
_____

What three qualities in your parents' marriage would you like to duplicate in your marriage?
1) _____
2) _____
3) _____

What three aspects of your parents' marriage would you not want to duplicate in your marriage?
1) _____
2) _____
3) _____

Describe any major marital crises in your parents' marriage:
The conflict(s) _____
_____
_____
_____

Reason for the conflict(s) _____
_____
_____
_____

Resolution of the conflict(s) _____
_____
_____
_____

Your feelings during the conflict(s) _____
_____
_____
_____

Are your feelings different now? Explain.

_____

_____

Were there any chemical dependency problems (drugs or alcohol) in your family (parents or siblings)?

Yes _____ No _____ If yes, how has that problem affected you?

_____

_____

Siblings
Name _____ Age _____
Residing in _____

Name _____ Age _____
Residing in _____

Name _____ Age _____
Residing in _____

Name _____ Age _____
Residing in _____

Name _____ Age _____
Residing in _____

Describe your relationship with your siblings during your childhood years:

_____

_____

_____

_____

_____

_____

_____

Dating History

How did you meet your fiancé(e)?

_____

_____

How long have you known each other?

_____

_____

How long have you been engaged?

_____

_____

Did you date others prior to meeting your fiancé(e)?
Yes ____ No ____ If yes, how many others have you dated?

_____

For how long? _____

Have you ever been engaged before? _____
If yes, did the prior engagement result in marriage? _____
If it did not, what ended the engagement?

_____

_____

Current Relationship

Do you and your fiancé(e) now love one another? _____
If yes, what do you mean when you say you "love" someone?

_____

_____

Why are you getting married? List five reasons in their order of
importance to you.
1) _____
2) _____
3) _____
4) _____
5) _____

What do you like about your fiancé(e)?
1) _____
2) _____
3) _____

What do you dislike about your fiancé(e)?
1) _____
2) _____
3) _____

In what ways do you think you will be a better person married than you could be by remaining single?

_____
_____
_____
_____

Describe what you believe should be the husband's role in marriage. Be as specific as possible.

_____
_____
_____
_____

Describe what you believe should be the wife's role in marriage. Be as specific as possible.

_____
_____
_____
_____

Briefly assess your current relationship.
Physically:

_____
_____
_____
_____

Emotionally:

_____

_____

Intellectually:

_____

_____

Spiritually:

_____

_____

Do you believe marriage is a covenant for life? _____
If yes, what steps are you taking to make this a lifetime commitment? _____

_____

_____

How do you communicate with each other?
From your perspective:

_____

_____

From your fiancé(e)'s perspective:

_____

_____

How do you resolve conflict?

_____

_____

_____

What is your view of:
Children in marriage:

_____

_____

_____

In-law relationships:

_____

_____

Two-career marriages:

_____

_____

Financial responsibility:
Do you enter this marriage in debt or with resources?

_____

_____

Have you discussed finances with each other?

_____

_____

Are you planning to have a prenuptial agreement?

_____

_____

Once you have completed this form, make a copy of it, return the original to the church, and exchange copies with your fiancé(e).

About the Author

Dan Chun is the senior pastor of First Presbyterian Church of Honolulu (fpchawaii.org). In 1983 he founded Hawaiian Islands Ministries (himonline.org) with his wife, Pam. With annual Honolulu spring gatherings of 4,000 adults and teenagers, the Chuns have trained more than 50,000 church leaders. A former journalist, Dan was a TV newscaster with a CBS affiliate in Honolulu. He has spoken all over the United States and in countries such as England, Thailand, China, Singapore and the Philippines. Dan received his M.A. from the University of Southern California in Cinema Production, and a M.Div. and a D.Min. from Fuller Theological Seminary where he is also a trustee. He is a rabid fan of Compassion International and The Alpha Course. You can follow Dan's blog at danchun.com. He and his wife have three children and two wonderful dogs, Max and Molly.

HowtoPickaSpouse.com